THE MOST
TRUSTED NAME
IN **TRAVEL**

Frommer's

↻ Shortcut

SWITZERLAND

...eresa Fisher,
...d Donald Strachan

FrommerMedia LLC

Published by
Frommer Media LLC

ISBN 978-1-62887-232-3 (paper), 978-1-32887-233-0 (e-book)

Editorial Director: Pauline Frommer
Editor: Elizabeth Heath
Production Editor: Erin Geile
Cartographer: Liz Puhl
Photo Editor: Meghan Lamb
Editorial Assistant: Ross F. Walker
For information on our other products or services, see www.frommers.com.

Frommer Media LLC also publishes its books in a variety of electronic formats. Some content that appears in print may not be available in electronic formats.

Manufactured in China

5 4 3 2 1

HOW TO CONTACT US

In researching this book, we discovered many wonderful places—hotels, restaurants, shops, and more. We're sure you'll find others. Please tell us about them, so we can share the information with your fellow travelers in upcoming editions. If you were disappointed with a recommendation, we'd love to know that, too. Please write to: Support@FrommerMedia.com

FROMMER'S STAR RATINGS SYSTEM

Every hotel, restaurant and attraction listed in this guide has been ranked for quality and value. Here's what the stars mean:

★ Recommended
★★ Highly Recommended
★★★ A must! Don't miss!

CONTENTS

LIST OF MAPS

AN IMPORTANT NOTE

ABOUT THE AUTHORS

Arthur Frommer is a graduate of the Yale University Law School, where he was an editor of the *Yale Law Journal,* and he is a member of the New York Bar. After service with U.S. Army Intelligence in Europe in the 1950s, he practiced law in New York with the law firm of the late Adlai Stevenson, but later embarked on the publication of travel guides, following the record-breaking success of his *Europe on $5 a Day,* which led to the creation—in partnership with his daughter—of one of the nation's leading publishers of travel guidebooks and travel websites, Frommers.com. He has subsequently written numerous other guidebooks, including several yearly editions of *The New World of Travel* exploring forms of alternative travel. He also co-hosts the nationally syndicated radio show *The Travel Show* with his daughter and writes an internationally syndicated newspaper column for King Features. He lives in New York City, where he has been an active trustee of the Community Service Society, the nation's leading anti-poverty organization.

Teresa Fisher is an author, photographer, and travel writer who has had a life-long love affair with Switzerland. She has written extensively for a variety of publishers including Frommer's, National Geographic, and Thomas Cook. She has also penned more than 30 guidebooks and children's travel reference books on a wide variety of destinations worldwide, and features periodically on BBC local radio as a travel advisor. Her travel features have appeared in such British publications as *The Daily Telegraph, The Sunday Telegraph* and *The Sunday Times.* She specialises in European cities, adventure travel, and all things Alpine, dividing her time between photojournalism and her family-oriented website, www.familyskinews.com.

Donald Strachan is a travel and technology journalist who has written about Italy for publications worldwide, including *National Geographic Traveller, The Guardian, Sydney Morning Herald,* and CNN.com.

ABOUT THE FROMMER TRAVEL GUIDES

For most of the past 50 years, Frommer's has been the leading series of travel guides in North America, accounting for as many as 24% of all guidebooks sold. I think I know why.

Though we hope our books are entertaining, we nevertheless deal with travel in a serious fashion. Our guidebooks have never looked on such journeys as a mere recreation, but as a far more important human function, a time of learning and introspection, an essential part of a civilized life. We stress the culture, lifestyle, history, and beliefs of the destinations we cover, and urge our readers to seek out people and new ideas as the chief rewards of travel.

We have never shied from controversy. We have, from the beginning, encouraged our authors to be intensely judgmental, critical—both pro and con—in their comments, and wholly independent. Our only clients are our readers, and we have triggered the ire of countless prominent sorts, from a tourist newspaper we called "practically worthless" (it unsuccessfully sued us) to the many rip-offs we've condemned.

And because we believe that travel should be available to everyone regardless of their incomes, we have always been cost-conscious at every level of expenditure. Though we have broadened our recommendations beyond the budget category, we insist that every lodging we include be sensibly priced. We use every form of media to assist our readers, and are particularly proud of our feisty daily website, the award-winning Frommers.com.

I have high hopes for the future of Frommer's. May these guidebooks, in all the years ahead, continue to reflect the joy of travel and the freedom that travel represents. May they always pursue a cost-conscious path, so that people of all incomes can enjoy the rewards of travel. And may they create, for both the traveler and the persons among whom we travel, a community of friends, where all human beings live in harmony and peace.

Arthur Frommer

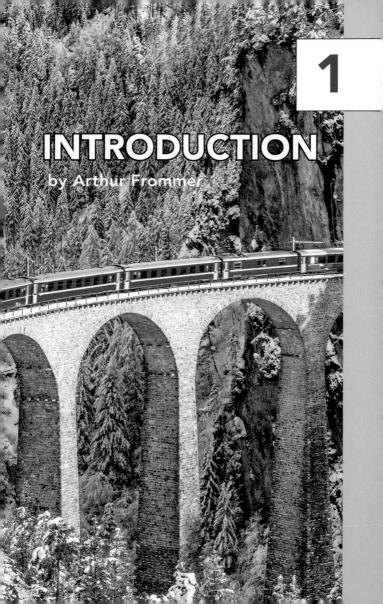

1

INTRODUCTION

by Arthur Frommer

Because of a widespread belief that the Swiss keep themselves aloof from the issues and problems confronting the rest of the world, a vacation in Switzerland can often seem a rather odd experience. It occurs among a people with a reputation—whether justified or not—for strongly isolationist attitudes. One hesitates to query them about their viewpoints on political or other serious matters.

An acquaintance of mine once summed up his understanding of that nation in the following analogy: pose a topic of politics to the average European, he said, and their eyes will light up with interest, their arms and hands will flail about, they will forcefully express an opinion. Pose the same question to most Swiss and, in his experience, their eyes will film over with boredom, and they will switch the subject to something trivial. They simply don't want to burden themselves with the cares afflicting other nations or other peoples.

That widespread belief about the Swiss is based, in part, on recent history, according to the same friend. Switzerland, the richest country on earth, with the highest per capita income, has made an almost religious commitment to neutrality. It refused to go to war, on either side, in both World Wars I and II. It has remained, since then, out of the European Community; it circulates its own currency, it failed even to join the United Nations until 2002, and it has evolved in such a different manner from the rest of us that it did not permit women to vote until 1971.

How much truth is there in the reputation of the Swiss as uninterested in what goes on elsewhere? I can't fully answer that question, because my own contact with Switzerland has been solely as a tourist with little opportunity to engage in personal discussions. But regardless of what others may feel, it is at least undeniable that the Swiss offer a superb touristic experience.

In addition to specializing in confidential commercial transactions (without asking questions), Switzerland has offered remarkable vacations to the hordes of foreigners who descend on it each year to go skiing or mountaineering in its breathtaking Alps. Prior to World War II, it was perhaps the most popular touristic destination in Europe, and although it later lost that position to beachfront resorts that could be reached easily by air, it still counts tourism as one of its most important sources of income.

Now where in Switzerland does the non-European visitor go for vacation pleasures? Many of us confine our stays to four cities: Lucerne, Zurich, Geneva, and Zermatt.

From a strictly touristic standpoint, German-speaking Lucerne (only 80,000 residents) is probably your best choice, for its cog-railway to the

Skiing in front of the Materhorn.

top of Mt. Pilatus and Mt. Rigi (commanding awesome views of the Alps), for its remarkable 14th-century wooden bridge, its touching monument of the "Dying Lion" (commemorating Swiss guards killed by Parisian activists during the French Revolution), and for its countless concerts and recitals in a music hall designed by the famous Jean Nouvel. Having myself vacationed there in recent years, I can vouch for its ability to calm and relax even the most stressed-out types.

For a very different stay of urban interest, we go to the much-larger Zurich, the financial, banking, and business capital of Switzerland. On its awesome Bahnhofstrasse, the city's main boulevard, we stroll a world-famous array of glitzy stores and offices. Elsewhere, we encounter a city of cultural riches (big theaters and concert halls, countless important museums) and of vast historical importance (here Zwingli led the Protestant Reformation of the 1500s). We take public transportation out onto the city's lake and river, and then into the heights overlooking it, from which one can view the nearby Alps. I have greatly enjoyed my own stays there, and have devoured more Swiss fondues in the city's excellent cafes than I care to remember.

French-speaking, expensive Geneva is the other largest city of Switzerland (bigger than Berne and Basel, and second in size only to Zurich), the home of numerous international government organizations whose sophisticated staffs patronize its many superb restaurants and theaters. The building and assembly hall of the former League of Nations is now the European headquarters of the United Nations, and numerous UN agencies are located here, as is the headquarters of the international Red Cross. It is no wonder that nearly half its population are resident foreign nationals, who enjoy the countless museums, theaters and concert halls in this graceful and elegant place. It makes for an interesting stop in your European tour.

As for tiny Zermatt (less than 6,000 residents), totally devoted to tourism and skiing, it is famous because it is entirely surrounded by the highest mountain peaks in Switzerland (some 15,000 ft. high), including the renowned Matterhorn, which dozens of adventurers have died attempting to climb (don't try it). The altitude is such that you can ski here year around (with some difficulty in summer). Many visitors claim their travels are complete once they have stayed in Zermatt.

And now you'll read what our Frommer expert says about Switzerland. Enjoy it!

2

ZURICH

by Teresa Fisher

Zurich is Switzerland's largest and most stylish city, majestically located on the northern shore of Zürichsee (Lake Zurich). It is a dynamic, fun-loving metropolis—a classy, classical city with a contemporary edge, preserving its architectural and cultural heritage yet surprising the world with the latest innovations in art and architecture, music, fashion and design.

Over the decades, the Confederation's long tradition of neutrality has attracted money into Zurich from around the world, and so the Swiss business and finance capital is justifiably famed for its unsurpassed banking prowess.

This generated affluence has also diffused throughout the city to create a self-confident, glossy urban environment. Indeed, today's Zurich is far removed from the old, dull, stereotypical image of staid bankers and precision timing, of little more than gold bars and chocolate bars . . . after all, this is the city that saw the birth of Dadaism—the very antithesis of conformity.

Throw in a generous handful of world-class art and music venues; some of the most luxurious shopping in Europe; vibrant, avant-garde nightlife which claims Europe's highest number of nightclubs per capita; and the infections joie de vivre of the Zürcher people, and it's no surprise that Switzerland's "little big city" frequently comes out top of the charts as one of Europe's most popular cities for quality of life—large

FACING PAGE: **Credit Suisse building in Paradeplatz Square.**

enough to offer world-class facilities yet small enough to retain its intimate Swiss charm.

Essentials

The Zurich Tourist Service website, **www.zuerich. com**, provides useful brochures, maps and apps plus a free hotel booking service and city tours.

ARRIVING Kloten Airport (www.zurich-airport.com; ℡ **043/816 22 11**) is Zurich's international airport, and the biggest airport in Switzerland. From here, it costs around CHF70 by taxi to travel to the city center, approximately 11 km (7 miles) south of the airport. You are better off catching a train from the airport railway station, which adjoins the airport. Direct trains to the city's main railway station, Zürich Hauptbahnhof, take less than 15 minutes and cost CHF11/6.60 (first/ second class one-way). Trains run every 15 to 30 minutes between 5:02am and 12:41am. Some hotels near the airport offer a free shuttle-bus or pick-up service.

The main **train station, Zürich Hauptbahnhof,** has good links with many European cities. There

Zurich cityscape.

are frequent high-speed trains from Munich to Zurich (journey time around 4 hr.) and four direct trains daily from Paris (journey time around 4 hr.); plus good connections from Salzburg (5½ hr.) and Vienna (8½ hr.). The best connection to Italy is via Milan (4 hr.). Within Switzerland, it takes just under one hour to Lucerne; just over one hour to Bern; and around three hours to Geneva. Contact **SBB** (**Swiss Federal Railways;** www.sbb.ch; ✆ **0900/300 300**) for schedules. From the Hauptbahnhof, at the heart of city center, it's easy to walk or to hop on a tram or bus to most Zurich hotels (see "Getting Around," facing page).

If **driving** from Geneva, take A1 northeast, via Bern, and on to Zurich; from Basel, follow the A3 eastward, connecting with the A1 into Zurich.

Buses from London, Paris, and other cities arrive at the main bus station at the city-center **Sihlquai terminal** in Limmatstrasse via **Eurolines** (www.eurolines.com; ✆ **227/169 120**).

CITY LAYOUT   Zurich is situated on Lake Zurich in northeast Switzerland, in a broad valley between the wooded slopes of the Zürichberg, Käferberg and Üetliberg hills. The city, and the **Altstadt (Old Town)** at its heart, is bisected into two main areas by the River Limmat. The left or West Bank, generally known as the **City Center,** contains the major slice of the Altstadt (Old Town) plus the legendary **Bahnhofstrasse** luxury shopping boulevard (see p. 46) and the **City** business and banking sector. The right or East Bank is characterized by the cobbled pedestrian district of **Niederdorf** which, with its village-like charm, provides a perfect counterpart to the glitzy, glamorous city center.

the ZÜRICHCARD

If you are planning a short visit to Zurich, the ZürichCARD (**www. zuerich.com/en/visit/your-city-travel-pass**) is an excellent value, especially if you're planning on visiting several museums. It provides free travel from the airport to the city and back; free public transport in the city; a free short round trip on Lake Zurich; free travel to the **Üetliberg ★★** (see p. 27) and back; free entry to most city museums (including the **Landesmuseum ★★★** [see p. 22] and the **Kunsthaus ★★★** [see p. 25]); a 50% discount on guided city tours with Zurich Tourism; plus a host of further discounts. A 24-hour pass costs CHF24 (or CHF16 for children); a 72-hour pass costs CH48/32 (adult/child). The ZurichCARD is available from Zurich Airport, the city tourist office, all railway stations in and around Zurich, various Zurich hotels, and city train and tram automated ticket machines.

GETTING AROUND   Zurich's city center can be easily explored on foot. To discover the suburbs, there's a comprehensive public transport system that will get you around easily.

Zurich's **public transport** system is operated by the Verkehrsbetriebe Zürich (Zurich Public Transport; www.vbz.ch; ✆ **0848/988 988**), and comprises an easy-to-use, ultra-efficient network of buses, boats, trains, and trams.

There's a bus or tram stop roughly every 300 meters in the city center, and you seldom have to wait longer than 5 minutes for a connection during the day. Most routes pass through the main train station (Hauptbahnhof) at the heart of town, and run daily between the hours of 5:30am and 12:30am.

You can buy tickets from automatic vending machines located at every stop. You must have a ticket and validate it in a ticket-puncher at the stop before you board any vehicle. Tickets are regularly controlled, and if you're caught without one, you'll pay a hefty fine. The basic fare on all buses and trams is CHF4.30 for a trip lasting no more than 1 hour. Better value is a Tageskarte (1-day ticket), which costs CHF8.60 and allows you to travel on all city buses and trams for 24 hours. Children up to age 6 can ride for free with a fare-paying adult. Maps of the transport network and timetables are displayed at all bus and tram stations.

Taxis are extremely expensive. Expect to pay CHF6 before you've even gotten into the vehicle, plus a further CHF3.80 per kilometer driven. There are

---

"Zu Reich"

There's no denying the Swiss are an affluent nation, and it's in Zurich that the serious money begins. After all, Zurich is Switzerland's financial engine, and boasts the world's fourth-biggest stock exchange. Most major Swiss banks have their headquarters in or around **Paradeplatz** (Parade Square).

The scene of a medieval market until the 19th century, then the main venue for military processions, nowadays Paradeplatz is better known now as a major tram intersection and the location of **Sprüngli ★★** (see p. 41), the city's ultimate café

experience serving the finest cakes, chocolates, and pâtisseries in the land.

It's ironic to think the vaults of gold that power Switzerland's banking capital lie just beneath the square and also in neighboring **Bahnhofstrasse** (see p. 46) where, at street level, the wealthy, fur-clad locals are happy to splash out on extravagant clothes, watches, jewelry and chocolates in some of Europe's most expensive boutiques. No wonder Zurich is sometimes nicknamed "Zu reich" ("too rich").

Cycling in Zurich.

several taxi stands where you can catch a cab, including Bürkliplatz by the lake and at the main railway station, or you can order a taxi by phone on © **044/444 4444.**

I don't recommend attempting to see Zurich **by car.** Once you're installed in your hotel, leave the car at a garage. Zurich can get very congested with traffic, parking is scarce and expensive, and the one-way systems are prevalent and sometimes baffling.

Cycling is a terrific way of getting around Zurich (except in winter when the cycle-paths can be icy), especially if you're planning on exploring the lake area beyond the city center. Bicycles can be rented at the baggage counter of the main train station (Hauptbahnhof; www.rentabike.ch; © **051/2222904**) for CHF35/27 per day/half-day. Hours are Monday to Friday, 7:30am to 7:45pm; weekends 8am to 7pm. You can also hire **Züri Rollt** bikes for free (with the presentation of a valid ID and a deposit of CHF20;

www.schweizrollt.ch) from various locations, including the Landesmuseum (see p. 22), Bellevue, Enge station and outside Globus City department store in Bahnhofstrasse from May to October.

The Neighborhoods in Brief

ALTSTADT (OLD TOWN)   The main Altstadt neighborhood clings to the west bank of the Limmat river. It is a picturesque maze of steeply cobbled streets containing some of the city's most beautiful medieval wooden-framed houses, many adorned with cascading geraniums, as well as a mass of tiny restaurants and boutiques. At its heart, on a small hill near the river bank, the tiny, tranquil **Lindenhof** quarter affords one of the best panoramas of Zurich from Lindenhofplatz—the original site of the Romans who first settled here in 15 B.C.

Old Town Zurich.

CITY   This neighborhood lies to the west of the Altstadt, and is centered on Zurich's grand tree-lined main thoroughfare, **Bahnhofstrasse**—one of the world's most famous shopping streets (see p 46)—which runs parallel to the river from the main station at **Bahnhofplatz** down to the lake. The main financial and business district spreads out from **Paradeplatz** westward and toward the lake. The northwest of the City district is fringed by the river Sihl, a small tributary of the Limmat. The predominantly residential neighborhood of **Aussersihl** lies beyond.

ENGE & WOLLISHOFEN The western shore of Lake Zurich is dominated by grassy parks, lakeside promenades, and turn-of-the-century mansions. In summer months, when everyone flocks to the lake to swim and relax, you'll find this side less crowded than the eastern Seefeld side. Stroll beyond Mythenquai and, before you know it, you'll be out in the countryside.

NIEDERDORF The quaint Niederdorf neighborhood, on the right bank of the River Limmat, forms the eastern half of the city's Altstadt, with its historic guildhall buildings lining the river quaysides. Beyond, a hilly maze of cobbled, pedestrianized lanes hide medieval buildings painted in pretty pastel shades, and shaded fountain-splashed squares full of trendy bars, attractive cafes, and quirky shops. Here too is the red-light district and the Grossmünster church (see p. 24), a veritable city landmark with its enormous twin towers. Above the Niederdorf is the **Hochschulen** district with its grandiose architecture and Switzerland's top gallery, the **Kunsthaus** (see p. 25), and the **University** district beyond.

SEEFELD South of the Niederdorf, the Seefeld district, with its grand belle Epoque architecture, is one of the most desirable (and pricey) residential districts of town—on the eastern shore of the lake. This neighborhood boasts the **Operahouse** (see p. 47) and plenty of stylish bars and restaurants, but its main draw is undoubtedly the lake and its attractive promenade, which runs along the grassy shoreline to

Zürichhorn Park, past lidos, boat hire venues, an open-air cinema, cafes, museums, and ornamental gardens.

ZÜRI WEST The once seedy, former industrial quarter of Zurich, northwest of the railway station, has undergone radical change and is now Zurich's fastest-developing business and residential district. Most striking are its numerous architectural projects, with derelict old factories and industrial buildings converted into trendy housing and cultural and entertainment spaces. With a thriving subculture and a multitude of bars, clubs, and restaurants springing up, Züri West has become the main focus of Zurich's hip party scene.

Exploring Zurich

Zurich is surprisingly easy to explore on foot, as most of the key sights lie within a compact area on either side of the River Limmat. The quays with their promenades and magnificent buildings are delightful for strolling, or for simply sitting at a cafe terrace, watching the world go by. Where the river opens onto the lake, you'll find Zurich's most impressive churches: **Fraumünster** (see below) and **Peterskirche ★** (see p. 19) on the west bank, and the **Grossmünster ★★** (see p. 24) on the east bank. Their spires also come in useful for navigation purposes, should you lose your bearings! From here, it's just a short walk to most of the city museums and galleries.

Many of Switzerland's finest museums are located here, including its premier gallery, the **Kunsthaus ★★★** (see p. 25), and the **Landesmuseum ★★★** (Swiss National Museum; see p. 22), which traces the fascinating history of the Confederation from pre-history to the present.

Zurich also claims magnificent **Lake Zurich** for recreation; some of Switzerland's finest restaurants; its best nightlife; and its most sophisticated shopping (famed especially for its haute couture, design, watches, jewelry, and chocolate).

ALTSTADT

Fraumünster ★★★ RELIGIOUS SITE This church, with its slender and distinctive turquoise spire, is well worth a visit. It is on the left bank overlooking Münsterhof, a historic old square on the site of a Benedictine abbey. It was founded here in 853 by Emperor Ludwig, the grandson of Charlemagne. His daughter became the first abbess. The present church dates from the 13th and 14th centuries, and the crypt of the old abbey church is preserved in the undercroft.

The Fraumünster is also celebrated for its elaborate organ. The basilica has three aisles; the nave is

Fraumünster and its turquoise spire.

in the Gothic style. The real draw, however, is a set of five **stained-glass windows**—each with its own color theme—designed by Marc Chagall. They are best seen in bright morning light.

Münsterhof. www.fraumuenster. ch. ℭ **044/211 41 00.** Free. Tram: 4 to City Hall. May–Sept Mon–Sat 9am–noon, daily 2–6pm; Oct and Mar–Apr Mon–Sat 10am–noon, daily 2–5pm; Nov–Feb Mon–Sat 10am–noon, daily 2–4pm.

Interior of Peterskirche, Zurich's oldest church.

Peterskirche (St Peter's Church) ★ RELIGIOUS
SITE   Built in the 13th century, St. Peter's—on the left bank south of Lindenhof—is the oldest church in Zurich. It also boasts the largest clock face in Europe: 9m (30 ft.) in diameter; the minute hand alone is almost 4m (13 ft.) long. Inside, the choir is Romanesque, but the three-aisle nave is baroque.

St. Peterhofstatt 1. www.st-peter-zh.ch. *℃* **044/211 25 88.** Free. Mon–Fri 8am–6pm; Tram 6, 7, 11, 13 (Rennweg). Sat 10am–4pm; Sun noon–5pm.

Zunfthaus zur Meisen ★ MUSEUM   The 18th-century "Winegrowers' Guildhall" is one of the city's most beautiful guild houses, facing the river and backing onto Münsterplatz, an attractive cobbled square which was once site of an ancient pig market. The ornate rococo interiors of the first floor, with their rich gold and stucco embellishments, provide an atmospheric

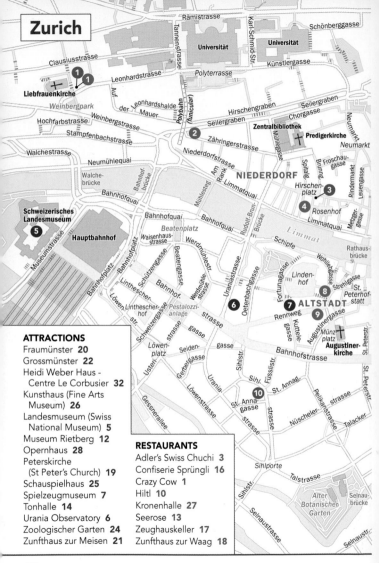

Zurich

Universität
Universität

Rämistrasse
Schönberggasse
Karl-Schmid-Str.
Tannenstrasse
Künstlergasse
Clausiusstrasse
Leonhardstrasse
Polyterrasse
Auf der Mauer
Leonhardshalde
Liebfrauenkirche
Weinbergpark
Hirschengraben
Seilergraben
Chorgasse
Weinbergstrasse
Neumarkt
Hochfarbstrasse
Weinbergstrasse
Polybahn (funicular)
Zentralbibliothek
Predigerkirche
Stampfenbachstrasse
Zähringerstrasse
Neumarkt
Walchestrasse
Neumühlequai
Niederdorfstrasse
NIEDERDORF
Walche-brücke
Bahnhof-brücke
Am Rank
Mühlegasse
Spitalg.
Brunng.
Froschaugasse
Bahnhofquai
Limmatquai
Hirschen-platz
Rindermarkt
Leuengasse
Schweizerisches Landesmuseum
Bahnhofquai
Bahnhofquai
Mühlesteg
Rosenhof
Limmatquai
Metzger-gasse
Hauptbahnhof
Museumstrasse
Beatenplatz
Rudolf-Brun-Brücke
Limmat
Schipfe
Rathaus-brücke
Bahnhofplatz
Waisenhaus-strasse
Werdmühlestr.
Uraniastrasse
Wohllebg.
Strehlgasse
St. Peterhof-statt
Bahnhofplatz
Schützengasse
Beatengasse
Werdmühle-strasse
Fortunagasse
Lindenhof
ALTSTADT
Bahnhof
Linthescher-hof
Linthescher-gasse
Löwen-str.
Pestalozzi-anlage
Oetenbachgasse
Rennweg
Kuttele-gasse
Augustinergasse
Lintheschergasse
Schweizergasse
Löwen-platz
Seiden-gasse
gasse
Münz-platz
Augustiner-kirche
St. Peterstr.
Usteristr.
Gerbergasse
Bahnhofstrasse
Gessneralle
Uraniastrasse
Löwenstrasse
Sihlstr.
Füsslistr.
St. Annag.
Pelikanstrasse
St. Peterstr.
St. Anna-gasse
St. Annagasse
Nüschelerstrasse
Talacker
Sihlstr.
Sihl
Urania
Sihlporte
Talstrasse
Alter Botanischer Garten
Selnau-brücke
Selnaustrasse
Selnaustr.

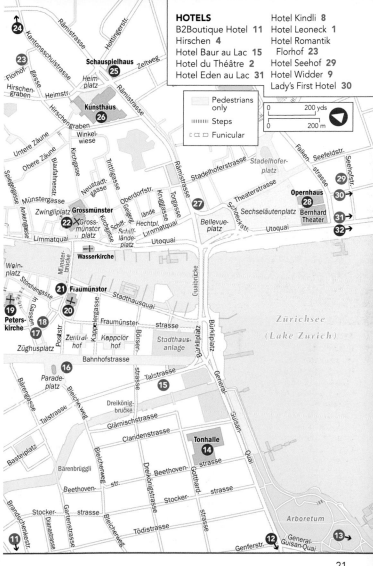

setting for the Swiss National Museum's collection of porcelain and faience, the majority of which was manufactured in Zurich's own porcelain factory in Kilchberg-Schooren during the 17th and 18th centuries. Be sure to see the delicate figurines, so charmingly grouped by theme—the seasons, the elements, love, hunting, and, of course, wine.

Münsterhof 20. www.zunfthaus-zur-meisen.ch. ⓒ **044/221 21 44.** CHF3; free for children 16 and under. Tram 2, 6, 7, 8, 9, 11, 13 (Paradeplatz). Thurs–Sun 11am–4pm.

CITY

Landesmuseum (Swiss National Museum) ★★★

MUSEUM   This sprawling museum contains the world's largest collection of Swiss historical and cultural artifacts, documenting civilization here from prehistory to the modern age. As you enter the museum, one of the first highlights is the gigantic scale model of

Interior, Landesmuseum.

the Battle of Murten, which most children adore. Beyond, you'll find everything Swiss imaginable from silver to stained glass, and from altarpieces to armor. It's worth getting an iPad tour (available at the entrance with a deposit of a passport or other personal ID) to help you navigate through the high-tech galleries. Highlights include children's toys, Renaissance globes, clock-making, regional costumes, and the characterful collections of artifacts from each of the country's cantons. Don't try to see everything—just pick two or three topics of particular interest, or check out the dynamic temporary exhibitions, and do take a break in the funky museum cafe for a reviving coffee and a scrumptious slice of cake.

Museumstrasse 2. www.musee-suisse.ch. ✆ **044/218 65 11.** CHF10 adults, free for children 16 and under. Tram 4, 11, 13, 14 (Bahnhofquai). Tues, Wed, and Fri Sun 10am–5pm, Thurs 10am–7pm.

ENGE & WOLLISHOFEN

Museum Rietberg ★★ MUSEUM   This is Switzerland's only gallery for non-European cultures, and it's world-renowned for its remarkable collections from Asia, Africa, the Americas, and Oceania—the majority donated to the city by banker and art patron Baron Eduard von der Heydt in 1952. Highlights of the vast collection are housed in Villa Wesendonck (an elegant neoclassical mansion once home to composer Richard Wagner); in the quirky redbrick Park-Villa Rieter; and within a maze of underground galleries cleverly built to enlarge the museum without altering its elegant appearance, apart from the addition of a striking "Emerald" glass foyer. Think Native American art, Middle Eastern textiles, Japanese Noh masks, early Buddhist sculptures from China . . . this museum provides a fascinating whistle-stop tour around the cultures of the world.

Gablerstrasse 15. www.rietberg.ch. © **044/415 31 31.** Adults CHF14, free for children 16 and under. Tram 7 (Museum Rietberg). Fri–Tues 10am–5pm, Wed–Thurs 10am–8pm.

NIEDERDORF

Grossmünster ★★ RELIGIOUS SITE This Romanesque and Gothic cathedral was, according to legend, founded by Charlemagne, whose horse bowed down on the spot marking the graves of three early Christian martyrs (see box facing page). The edifice has two three-story towers and is situated on a terrace above Limmatquai, on the right bank. Construction began in 1090 and additions were made until the early 14th century.

The choir contains stained-glass windows completed in 1932 by Augusto Giacometti. (Augusto is not

The Grossmünster.

to be confused with his more celebrated uncle, Alberto Giacometti, the famous Swiss abstract artist.) In the crypt is a weather-beaten, 15th-century statue of Charlemagne, a copy of which crowns the south tower.

The cathedral was once the parish church of Huldrych Zwingli, one of the great leaders of the Reformation. In accordance with Zwingli's beliefs, Zurich's Grossmünster is austere, stripped of the heavy ornamentation you'll find in the cathedrals of Italy. The view from the towers is impressive.

Grossmünsterplatz. www.grossmuenster.ch. © **044/252-59-49.** Free admission to cathedral; towers 4F. Tram: 4. Cathedral Mar 15–Oct daily 10am–6pm; Nov–Mar 14 daily 10am–5pm. Towers (weather permitting) Mar–Oct daily 10am–5pm; Nov–Feb Sat–Sun 10am–5pm.

Kunsthaus ★★★ MUSEUM   The airy, lofty, glassy galleries of Switzerland's top art museum house art treasures spanning six centuries, from the Middle Ages to the present, but the main focus is on 19th- and 20th-century art, with works by all the greats, including Bonnard, Braque, Cézanne, Chagall, Degas, Mondrian, Monet, and Picasso. There are also some magnificent early Impressionist canvases by lesser-known Swiss artists such as Ferdinand Hodler and Giovanni Segantini, and some key works of Swiss Realism and Zurich Concrete Art. The Kunsthaus also contains the largest collection of works by Edvard Munch outside Scandinavia, and the world's finest collection of works by celebrated Swiss artist, sculptor, and graphic artist Alberto Giacometti. The Kunsthaus is undergoing major redevelopment with the addition of new exhibition spaces and an art garden, so some displays may be closed. If you are interested in a

Headless Saints

The Grossmünster is dedicated to the city's patron saints, Felix, Regula and Exuperantius. In the 3rd century, the three martyrs attempted to convert the citizens of Turicum (the original name for Zurich) to Christianity. According to legend, the governor had them plunged into boiling oil and forced them to drink molten lead. The trio refused to renounce their faith and were beheaded. Miraculously, they still had enough energy to pick up their heads and climb to the top of a hill (the present site of the cathedral), where they dug their own graves and then interred themselves. The seal of Zurich honors these saints, depicting them carrying their heads under their arms. Their remains are said to rest in one of the chapels of the cathedral.

particular collection, call ahead or check the website to make sure it's on view.

Heimplatz 1. www.kunsthaus.ch. © **044/253 84 84.** CHF15 adults (with audioguide), free for kids 16 and under. Tram 3, 5, 8, 9 (Kunsthaus). Tues 10am–6pm, Wed–Fri 10am–8pm, Sat–Sun 10am–6pm.

SEEFELD

Heidi Weber Haus—Center Le Corbusier ★

MUSEUM "A house is a machine for living in" once said the renowned Swiss architect and visual artist Le Corbusier. And so he built the Heidi Weber Haus to embody his maxim of ideological formalism, commissioned by the art patron Heidi Weber in the early 1960s but not complete until 2 years after Le Corbusier's death, in 1967.

Today this extraordinary edifice serves as a quirky museum of his life and works—the culmination of his

ÜETLIBERG—top OF ZURICH

No visit to Zurich would be complete without a trip up the **Üetliberg ★★** (www.uetliberg.ch), dubbed the "top of Zurich" at an elevation of 871m/2,858 ft. In just 20 minutes (catch the S10 Sihltal Zurich-Üetliberg train from the Hauptbahnhof, platform 21 or 22, to Üetliberg station), you can escape from the jet-setting city into the lush meadows, tinkling cowbells, and chocolate-box landscapes which so epitomize Switzerland.

The Üetliberg marks the start of a popular 2-hour hiking route along a forested mountain ridge, with glorious 360-degree views over the city and the lake to the Alps beyond. Simply follow signs to Folsenogg, from where a cable car connects to Adliswil station and trains back to Zurich.

Even if you don't fancy the walk, it's still worth visiting the Üetliberg—there's a restaurant at the top (Gmüetliberg, Hotel Uto Kulm; ⓒ **044/463 92 60;** reservations advisable), just 7 minutes' walk from the train station, which serves mouth-watering seasonal fare and Swiss specialties too.

Zurich viewed from the top of the Üetliberg.

studies in architecture, interior design, and visual arts. Frustratingly, the interior is seldom open; do go inside if you get the chance. Otherwise, the exterior is also worth admiring if you're strolling by the lake—an eccentric cuboid of brass, concrete, and steel with bold, brightly colored enamel blocks and an oddly elevated, umbrella-like roof, which stands in stark contrast to the gentle parkland of its surrounds.

Höschgasse 8. www.centerlecorbusier.com. ℂ **044/383 64 70.** Bus 912, 916 (Chinagarten). July–Sept Sat–Sun 2–5pm.

Organized Tours

Forget guided bus tours of Zurich. The best way to discover the city is to get out and about in the fresh air. The Zurich Tourist Service Office offers a number of guided walking tours, as well as tours by bike, Segway, rickshaw, electric-scooter, even paddleboard, so choose your favorite mode of transport and climb aboard.

One of the most appealing **walking tours** in Zurich is a 2-hour guided stroll entitled **Stories of the Old Town,** which costs CHF25 for adults, CHF13 for children. It sets off from the main hall of the Hauptbahnhof at the Tourist Service Office (www.zuerich.com; ℂ **044/215 40 00;** daily Apr–Oct at

Credit Suisse building in Paradeplatz Square.

3pm, also weekends at 11am; Nov–March Wed, Sat, and Sun at 11am, also Sat at 3pm). For an alternative perspective, the evening **Ghost Walks** (www.ghost walk.ch) are highly entertaining. They take place Thursdays and Fridays at 8pm, starting at the fountain in Paradeplatz, and cost CH15 per person (not suitable for children under 14).

Zurich by Bike offers a weekly **Classic City** tour (www.zurichbybike.ch; CHF25 per person), which explores Züri West as well as the more mainstream sights of the city center, Sundays from May to October, from 10:30am to 1pm. It starts outside the **Züri Rollt** bike hire stand at the main railway station (see p. 10, advance booking is required).

The **Classic Trolley Tour** is a fun way to get your bearings, to learn about the history and lifestyle of the Zürichers, and to sightsee undercover if the weather is inclement. The tour starts at Bus-Parkplatz Sihlquai at 9:45am, midday and 2pm. It costs CHF34 for adults, CHF17 for kids (including multilingual commentary through personal earphones) and lasts 1½ to 2 hours.

The **Zürich Schifffahrtsgesellschaft** (Lake Zurich Navigation Company; www.zsg.ch) operates lake cruises throughout the year, as well as specialty cruises (see box below) and nostalgic paddle-steamer tours in summer months. **Limmatschifffahrt** boats (also operated by ZSG) shuttle up the Limmat river between the Landesmuseum and Bürkliplatz Pier on the lake twice an hour from April to October. The round trip takes approximately one hour and costs CHF4.30.

Especially for Kids

Zurich is a popular city for kids, with plenty of green spaces, especially around the lake, and over 80 playgrounds—ask your hotel to direct you to the one nearest to you. Children love visiting the **Üetliberg ★★** (see p. 27) and, in summer months, there's swimming and boats for hire on the lake and mini-cruises year-round (see above).

The **Zoologischer Garten (Zoological Gardens) ★★** (Zürichbergstrasse 221; www.zoo.ch; ✆ **044/254 25 00**) is one of the city's big crowd-pleasers for families young and old, with around 2,200 animals of about 260 species. It also contains a replica of a tropical rainforest, lodged within a state-of-the-art building which successfully replicates the temperatures, light levels, and humidity of Madagascar; while the Zoolino petting area is especially popular with toddlers.

Urania Observatory.

Other family-friendly highlights include the **Landesmuseum ★★★** (Swiss National Museum; p. 22) with its wide variety of hands-on displays; the **Urania Observatory ★★**, Uraniastrasse 9 (www.urania-sternwarte.ch; ✆ **044/211-65-23**) for budding star-gazers; and the tiny **Spielzeug Museum (Toy Museum) ★**, Fortunagasse 15 (www.zuercher-spielzeugmuseum.ch; ✆ **044/211 93 05**), a

ZÜRICHSEE—the city's blue lung

Zürichsee is the city's playground, with beautiful grassy parks, promenades and stately fin de siècle mansions set against a backdrop of snow-clad mountains. During summer, it's where the city's heart beats loudest, popular for strolling, sunbathing, boating, parkour trails, barbecuing, and swimming—the water is very clean and surprisingly warm, so be sure to bring your swimsuit.

No trip here is complete without a **mini-cruise** on the lake. **Zürichsee Schiff-fahrtsgesellschaft** (Lake Zurich Navigation Company), Mythenquai 333 (www.zsg.ch; ☏ **044/487 13 33**), offers a variety of excursions setting out daily from Bürkliplatz square. They range from 1½-hour mini-tours to romantic sunset cruises, jolly fondue evenings, and full-day outings. During summer, paddle-steamers ply between the towns and villages which dot the shoreline: Küsnacht is especially picturesque, and Rapperswil is also worth a visit for its many rose gardens; Circus Museum; and highly regarded children's zoo, Knies Kinderzoo. The countryside surrounding the lake with its lush, rolling hills, some clad in vineyards, is a hikers' paradise. It's also possible to explore the lake by train (the track runs the length of both shores, offering an easy, scenic journey), or by bicycle.

charming collection of toys dating from the 18th to the 20th centuries.

Several stores are also fun to visit with your kids, especially **Pastorini** (Weinplatz 3; www.pastorini.ch; ☏ **044/284 33 44**) is one of Zurich's biggest toy stores and is charmingly old-fashioned, with five floors brimming with quality toys, puppets, dolls houses, puzzles, board games, arts and crafts; and **Kinderbu-chladen Zürich** (Oberdorfstrasse 32; www.kinderbu chladen.ch; © **044/265 30 00**) is the best-stocked children's bookstore in Switzerland, with many English-language books.

Where to Stay

Zurich is an ideal city in which to become acquainted with Swiss hospitality. The city has more than 120 hotels to suit all tastes and budgets, from deluxe five-star palace-hotels (with price tags to match) to basic budget hotels. However, it can be difficult to find a room, because the top hotels are often filled with business travelers. So, if possible, make your booking well in advance. All the hotels listed here are within easy walking distance or just a short bus ride or tram-hop from the main Hauptbahnhof train station in the city center.

ALTSTADT
Expensive
Hotel Kindli ★ This cozy little townhouse hotel has been accommodating guests for more than 500 years. Located on a picturesque cobbled street in the pedestrian-only old town, the hotel manages to be quiet but still central. Every last detail has been considered in its 20 individually designed rooms, each fitted with country-house furnishings, right down to the specially "energized" water in the bathroom (it's like bathing in bottled mineral water and is supposedly very good for you). The superior rooms feature deluxe Swedish Hästens beds. The restaurant has an excellent reputation for its classic Swiss dishes.

Pfalzgasse 1. www.kindli.ch. © **043/888 76 76.** 20 units. Doubles CHF380–CHF440, included breakfast and minibar. Tram 6, 7, 11, 13 or 17 (Rennweg). **Amenities:** Restaurant; free Wi-Fi.

Hotel Widder ★★★ Old meets new at the luxurious and quirky Widder, made up of eight adjoining medieval houses and named after the 13th-century Augustinian monastery once located here. Thanks to careful restoration, the original stone walls, murals, frescoes, and ceilings have been preserved in the characterful interior. The rooms and suites are individually decorated with furniture and art from such luminaries as Le Corbusier, Mies van der Rohe, Frank Lloyd Wright, Giacometti, and Warhol; the interior schemes match the ice-cream shades of the eight exterior buildings. The restaurant serves top-notch Swiss and vegetarian cuisine; the Widder Bar is a celebrated jazz venue.

Rennweg 7. www.widderhotel.ch. ℂ **044/224 25 26**. 60 units. Doubles CHF650–CHF850, suites CHF1,050–CHF4,000. Tram 6, 7, 11, 13 or 17 (Rennweg). **Amenities:** spa; swimming pool; conference facilities; room service; free Wi-Fi.

CITY
Expensive
Hotel Baur au Lac ★★★ The Baur au Lac is one of Switzerland's grandest hotels. Set in private

Penthouse of Hotel Widder.

HÜRLIMANN SPA—bathing in beer

Perched on a hill, and a 10-minute ride by tram and bus from the city center, this boldly designed and very happening spa is housed inside the old **Hürlimann Brewery** of 1836—a striking building of whitewashed walls and towering brick chimneys. Within, the original wooden vats have been restored and converted into pools of varying temperatures, heated naturally from a nearby spring. The brewery's former barrel-vaulted stone chambers have been converted into auxiliary pools, steam rooms, and chill-out zones, but the pièce de résistance is undoubtedly the rooftop baths where you can soak up 360-degree city vistas from the vast open-air hot tub.

The adjoining **B2Boutique Hotel** is equally quirky, with its industrial chic bedrooms, its striking library lounge of floor-to-ceiling bookcases boasting 33,000 books, and a theatrical lobby which uses beer crates instead of coffee tables. Hotel guests pay just CHF25 (instead of the regular CHF55 per person) to bathe in the thermal bath complex (Brandschenkestrasse 150; www.thermalbad-zuerich.ch; www.b2boutiquehotels.com; ☏ **044/567 67 67**; tram 5, 8, 13, 17 [Bahnhof Enge/Bederstrasse], then bus 66 [Hürlimannplatz]).

parkland on the shores of Lake Zurich, at the head of the fashionable Bahnhofstrasse, it has the perfect location for shopping and sightseeing. The hotel has been owned by the same family since it opened in 1844, and it has welcomed royalty, celebrities, and discerning travelers with unequaled hospitality ever since. The beautifully appointed rooms, with sumptuous, classic furnishings, make all guests feel like celebrities, as does the excellent service. In summer

Hotel Baur au Lac.

months, meals are served in the garden, which overlooks the lake and the Alps beyond.

Talstrasse 1. www.bauraulac.ch. © **044/220 50 20.** 120 units. Doubles CHF870, suites CHF1,200. Tram 2, 8, 9 or 11 (Börsenstrasse or Bürkliplatz). **Amenities:** 3 restaurants; bars; business center; rooftop gym; room service; concierge; free Wi-Fi.

NIEDERDORF

Expensive

Hotel Romantik Florhof ★★★   Near the Kunsthaus art gallery (see p. 25), this secluded boutique hotel is in a genteel 15th-century merchant's house in a picturesque residential district that twists up from the quaint squares and cobbled alleys of the Niederdorf. The bedrooms are large and airy, and each is individually decorated with traditional English-countryhouse style furnishings and stylish, modern bathrooms. On the top (fourth) floor, the spacious, air-conditioned deluxe double room and junior suite, with its Jacuzzi, are the pick of the bunch. The elegant restaurant serves upmarket, seasonal Swiss fare and has an extensive list of Swiss wines. And the leafy patio garden here makes a nice break from the bustle of the city center in the summer.

Florhofgasse 4. www.florhof.ch. ☏ **044/250 26 26.** 35 units. Doubles CHF370–CHF430, suites CHF540–CHF670, includes breakfast Tram 3 (Neumarkt). **Amenities:** Restaurant; garden; free Wi-Fi.

Moderate

Hirschen ★★★ For location, it's hard to beat the Hirschen, which is at the heart of the fashionable Niederdorf district. It's also well priced and full of character—it's been a guesthouse since the 14th century, making it one of the city's oldest hotels. Today's simple, family-run hotel is kept in good repair, and although the rooms are pint-size, they are bright and functional without being generic, with crisp white bed linens. Some feature exposed ancient stonework, and one of the rooms has its own private roof terrace. In the basement is a wine cellar, the Weinschenke, with an excellent selection of Swiss and international wines.

Niederdorfstrasse 13. www.hirschen-zuerich.ch. ☏ **043/268 33 33.** 27 units. Doubles CHF200, includes breakfast. Tram 4, 9 11, 15 (Rudolf-Brun-Brücke). **Amenities:** Wine bar; roof terrace; free Wi-Fi.

Inexpensive

Hotel du Théâtre ★ It's hard to believe that this stylish B&B near the main railway station once housed a German-language theater in the 1950s. The most theatrical element nowadays is its modern glass entrance and lobby. The interior decor is simpler, but still stylish and comfortable. Alongside all the usual amenities, the rooms are furnished with a selection of novels, play scripts, poetry, philosophy, and audio books. The lounge often hosts book readings, harking back to the hotel's dramatic past.

Seilergraben 69. www.hotel-du-theatre.ch. ☏ **044/267 2670.** 50 units. CHF130 single, CHF180 double, breakfast CHF23 extra. Tram 3-7, 10-11 0r 13-15 (Central). **Amenities:** Restaurant; lounge; free Wi-Fi.

Hotel Leoneck ★★　This adorable and fun hotel, which has been decorated in "Swiss ethnic" style, is a good choice for families. There are cows everywhere: cow ornaments, cowbells, and cow upholstery. The staff is friendly and helpful, and the rooms are bright, simple, and streamlined, with amusing design touches, original wall paintings by local artists, and Toblerone chocolates on your pillow at night. The adjoining **Crazy Cow ★★** restaurant (see p. 45) continues the Swiss-kitsch theme. Situated to the northwest of Niederdorf, Tram 10 will bring you directly from the airport or main train station right to the front door.

Leonhardstrasse 1. www.leoneck.ch. ⓒ **044/254 22 22.** 80 units. Doubles CFH160–CHF250, family rooms CHF300–CHF400. Rates include breakfast. Trams 7, 6, 10, 15 (Haldenegg). **Amenities:** Restaurant; free Wi-Fi.

SEEFELD

Expensive

Hotel Eden au Lac ★★★　Set on the shores of Lake Zurich, a few steps from the Opera and a 10-minute walk from Bahnhofstrasse, the five-star Eden au Lac is one of the city's finest hotels. A gem built in 1909, it's got old world charm and elegance— from its bedrooms, furnished in neo-baroque style, to its Art Nouveau banquet halls. The French restaurant here is famed for its hot hors d'oeuvres—one of the earliest tasting menus—which were developed here for the Aga Khan III during his stay during World War II. Today's reincarnation comprises six courses and costs CHF145. Our favorite experience is in winter, when the Top of Eden roof terrace provides hot water bottles and blankets with its fondue menu to allow for

Hotel Eden au Lac.

cold-weather enjoyment of its unsurpassed lake and city views.

Utoquai 45. www.edenaulac.ch. ⓒ **044/266 2525.** 56 units. Doubles CHF650. Tram 2, 4, 5, 9, 11 (Kreuzstrasse). **Amenities:** 3 restaurants; bar; conference facilities; room service; concierge; free Wi-Fi.

Moderate

Hotel Seehof ★★   Given its close proximity to the opera and the shores of Lake Zurich, this hotel is an excellent value; it's a favorite of in-the-know business travelers—and opera singers. The pink facade of the 1930s townhouse it's in belies a radically modern interior of minimalist white walls, varnished oak floors, trendy furniture, and works by young local artists. The popular bar contains an excellent selection of wines and enhances the generally hip vibe.

Seehofstrasse 11. www.seehof.ch. ⓒ **044/254 57 57.** 20 units. Doubles CHF145–CHF370, suites CHF270–CHF430. Tram: 2, 4, 5, 9 or 11 (Opernhaus). **Amenities:** Restaurant; bar; free minibar; free Wi-Fi.

Lady's First Hotel ★★ This elegant boutique hotel is in a smart residential district, just a stone's throw from the lake and the city center. It's within a 19th-century building that was once a finishing school for young ladies, so it seems fitting that when it first opened in 1994, the hotel was for women only. The spa and the top floors remain that way, although men can get in-room massages in the stylish bedrooms, some of which have balconies overlooking the lake. Expect sleek, contemporary furnishings, high ceilings, parquet floors, and the occasional bold accent of color. A tempting evening menu of Italian dishes is served in the restaurant, garden, or lounge. There's a cozy log fire in winter, and a rose garden in summer, but the crowning glory of the hotel year-round is the roof terrace, which comes with beautiful skyline vistas.

Mainaustrasse 24. www.ladysfirst.ch. **℃ 044/380 80 10.** 28 units. Doubles CHF290, suites CHF325. Rates include breakfast. Tram 4 (Feldeggstrasse). **Amenities:** Spa; roof terrace; free Wi-Fi.

Where to Eat

Zurich restaurants feature a selection of both international and Swiss specialties. One local favorite is *rösti* (potatoes grated and fried). You should also try *Züri-Gschnätzlets* (shredded veal cooked with mushrooms in a cream sauce laced with white wine) and *Kutteln nach Zürcherart* (tripe with mushrooms, white wine, and caraway seed). Another classic dish is *Leberspiesschen* (liver cubes skewered with bacon and sage and served with potatoes and beans).

Among local wines, the white Riesling Sylvaner is outstanding and great with fish. The light Clevner wines, always chilled, are made from blue Burgundy grapes that grow around the lake. You should be able to order wine by the glass, even in first-class restaurants.

ALTSTADT
Expensive
Zunfthaus zur Waag ★★★ SWISS   The "Weavers' Guildhall" is without a doubt one of the most stylish restaurants in town. Inside a 17th-century hall near the river, its series of wood-paneled Biedermeier-style dining rooms make an intimate, candlelit spot for dining on top-notch local specialties, which are enhanced by the exemplary service. The menu usually includes *Zürcher Geschnetzeltes* (sliced veal in a mushroom cream sauce) with crisp *rösti* (potato cakes); and fried filets of perch straight from the lake, served with almond butter. Reservations are a very good idea.

Markthalle im Viadukt, Münsterhof 8. www.zunfthaus-zur-waag. ch. **044/216 99 66.** Mains CHF41–CHF56. Tram 2, 6–9, 11, 13 (Paradeplatz). Daily 11:30am–2pm and 6pm–10pm.

CITY
Moderate
Hiltl ★★★ VEGETARIAN   When it opened way back in 1898, Hiltl was Europe's first vegetarian restaurant; more than a hundred years later, it remains Zurich's top vegetarian option, with daily changing seasonal menus. Plan on eating early, or expect to wait in line for the impressive salad bar of 100 homemade dishes (you pay by the weight, per 100g, or about 3.5 oz.). At lunchtime, you can order the dish of the day for CHF20, and add soup or salad to it for an extra CHF3. Or tuck into a copious bowl of pasta, a chili-bean casserole, or one of the daily curry specialties. The spicy Malaysian Rendang and the Paneer Makhani are two of our favorites, or there's a curry

buffet for those who can't decide (pay per 100g at lunchtime, or a fixed price at dinner). Wash it all down with freshly squeezed juices, or homemade iced teas and yogurt-based lassis. There is also a limited wine and beer list. The neighboring Hiltl deli serves great coffees, juices, and vegetarian takeout for those in a hurry.

Sihlstrasse 28. www.hiltl.ch. ✆ **044/227 70 00.** Mains CHF20–CHF36, breakfast buffet (served Mon–Fri 6am–10:30am, Sat 6am–12:30pm) CHF29, Sunday brunch CHF57. Tram 2, 6–9, 11, 13 (Paradeplatz). Mon–Wed 6am–midnight or later, Sun 8am–midnight.

Zeughauskeller ★★ SWISS   Zurich's top beer hall was used to store weapons in the 15th century; these days it's packed instead with wooden tables (and you might be asked to share one with other guests in true, sociable, beer-cellar fashion). Expect a lively atmosphere, old-fashioned Bavarian-style oom-pah music, and massive steins of local beer, all drawn straight from the barrel. The wholesome Swiss fare includes 15 different sausage dishes, all served with a dollop of sauerkraut. The meter-long Kanonenputzer ("Cannon Cleaner") sausage feeds four.

Bahnhofstrasse 28a (main entrance around the corner at In Gassen) www.zeughauskeller.ch. ✆ **044/220 15 15.** Mains CHF19–CHF35, set menu CHF35. Tram 2, 6–9, 11 or 13 to Paradeplatz. Daily 11:30–11pm.

Inexpensive
Confiserie Sprüngli ★★ CAFE   The extravagant window displays here are good at luring customers into what is Switzerland's top confectionary and chocolate shop, at the hub of its most exclusive shopping boulevard. Less well-known to tourists, however, is the elegant cafe upstairs, where you can sip coffee served on a silver salver while rubbing shoulders with

Desserts from Confiserie Sprunglei.

the refined and well-to-do of Zurich. It's like winding the clocks back to the height of the city's Belle Epoque grandeur, with its old-fashioned manners and extravagant mirrors and gilt. The creamy cakes and fruit pastries are each a work of art; the seasonal salads and sandwiches make a perfect light lunch; don't leave without a box of Luxembourgli, Sprüngli's trademark bite-size macaroons.

Bahnhofstrasse 21, above the Sprüngli shop. www.spruengli. ch. © **044/224 46 16.** Sandwiches and salads CHF5.20–CHF14. Tram 2, 6–9, 11, 13 (Paradeplatz). Mon–Fri 7am–6:30pm, Sat 8am–6pm, Sun 9:30am–5:30pm.

ENGE & WOLLISHOFEN
Expensive
Seerose ★★ INTERNATIONAL In summer months, many of the city's fashionable boating crowd head to this chic lakeside hotspot, right on the shores of Lake Zurich. Book well in advance to ensure a table on the attractive lakeside deck, where there are giant

nautical-striped parasols. The waiting staff can be a bit snobbish and brusque at times, but the top-notch cuisine more than makes up for any shortfalls in service. The sublime beef tournedos is the signature dish here, although the fish dishes also come highly recommended, especially the grilled sole. The daily two-course lunch menu is a good value at CHF32, or you can opt for the Seerose's latest craze, an "anti-aging menu" for CHF37.

Seestrasse 493. www.dinning.ch. © **044/481 63 83**. Mains at lunch CHF18–CHF59, Mains at dinner CHF24–CHF74. Bus 161, 165 (Seerose). Lake club daily 9am–midnight. Lunch: 11:45am–1:45pm, dinner: 6–9:45pm.

NIEDERDORF

Expensive

Kronenhalle ★★ SWISS   Many say Kronenhalle is Zurich's top restaurant, but in fact this former beer hall is more than just a restaurant—it's a culinary landmark, the perfect blend of haute cuisine and fine art. Its intimate, old-world dining areas, with white linen tablecloths, soft candlelight, chandeliers, and dark-wood walls, are also bedecked with a breathtaking collection of paintings by Picasso, Rodin, Matisse, and Bonnard as well as stained glass by Chagall and furnishings by Giacometti. Ever since the restaurant opened in 1921, local politicians, businessmen, musicians, artists, and thinkers (including Sigmund Freud and Albert Einstein) have come here for a traditional menu of exemplary Swiss fare, which is served the old-fashioned way, from silver-domed serving dishes on side tables by elegant, white-frocked waiters. Signature dishes include a salad with Balleron sausage, followed by a chateaubriand steak and the richest of chocolate mousses. Advance reservations are strongly recommended: Ask for the table in the corner of the main dining room, beside a portrait of James Joyce—the author wrote large chunks of *Ulysses* while seated here.

Rämistrasse 4, off Limmatquai. www.kronenhalle.com. ✆ **044/ 262 99 00.** Mains CHF28–CHF68. Tram 2, 4, 5, 8, 9, 11, 15 (Bellevue). Daily noon–midnight.

Moderate

Adler's Swiss Chuchi ★★★ SWISS This simple, bright, chalet-style restaurant with traditional wood-clad walls transports its guests straight from the city to the Alps. It's an absolute must for all cheese fans. Alongside such popular local staples as Alpine macaroni (baked with lots of potatoes), meat fondues, and crispy rösti potato dishes, there are lots of raclette and fondue options. Our favorite is the "Farmers Fondue," with cheese, bacon, and cherry brandy. The wine menu is exclusively Swiss and broken down by

Enjoying fondue at Adler's Swiss Chuchi.

cantons—most are available by the glass as well as by the bottle. In summer months, you can eat outside, on the cobbled pavements of Niederdorf, the city's pedestrian-only medieval quarter. At the end of your meal, as a finishing touch, the bill is presented inside a music box.

Hotel Adler, Rosengasse 10. www.hotel-adler.ch. ☎ **044/266 9696.** Mains CHF21–CHF42. Tram 4, 15 (Rudolf-Brun-Brücke). Daily 11:30am–11:15pm.

Inexpensive
Crazy Cow ★★ SWISS   There's nothing refined about the Crazy Cow. From the kitschy wall paintings inspired by Swiss stereotypes (snowboarding cows, flying cuckoo clocks, trains, half-eaten Toblerone bars) to the virtually unintelligible menu, written in Swiss dialect, this lively restaurant certainly lives up to the first half of its name. But don't worry, the menu is translated into English, and you can be guaranteed a hearty, rustic meal of such traditional fare as rösti, Swiss-style macaroni casserole (with potatoes, bacon, and cheese), and *raclette* (cheese melted over a fire and then served over potatoes or bread).

Hotel Leoneck, Leonhardstrasse 1. www.crazycow.ch. ☎ **044/ 261 40 55.** Mains CHF19–CHF40. Trams 7, 6, 10, or 15 (Haldenegg; the tram stop is right outside the restaurant). Daily 6:30am–midnight.

Shopping
Zurich offers some of the finest shopping in all of Switzerland, and some of the most expensive in the world, with its dazzling selection of boutiques ranging from international haute couture and exclusive Swiss watches to beautifully handcrafted local souvenirs, not to mention more chocolate shops than is good for even the most devoted chocoholics.

The main shopping district occupies a square kilometer (about ⅓ sq. mile) at the heart of the city, centered on glitzy, car-free **Bahnhofstrasse,** one of the world's most celebrated and sophisticated shopping boulevards, stretching from the main train station to the lake. Here renowned confectioners, jewelers, and watchmakers jostle for space alongside haute-couture boutiques in the most overt manifestation of the nation's wealth.

The nearby tiny specialist shops of the hilly, cobbled Altstadt are also worth a browse, as is the tiny artisan quarter beside the river at Schipfe with its quirky antiquities shops. Across the river in the Niederdorf, you'll find a more eclectic, generally cheaper, and certainly quirkier array of boutiques, interior design shops, and galleries.

For that once-in-a-lifetime Swiss timepiece purchase, head to **Beyer,** Bahnhofstrasse 31 (www.beyer-ch.com; ☏ **043/344 63 63**), which also contains a small but fascinating **Clock & Watch Museum** in the basement. There's also a more modestly priced **Swatch** shop nearby, at Bahnhofstrasse 94 (www.swatch.ch; ☏ **044/221 28 66**).

Other shopping highlights include Swiss shoe institution **Bally** (Bahnhofstrasse 20; www.bally.ch; ☏ **044/224 39 39**); **Schweizer Heimatwerk** (Uraniastrasse 1; www.heimatwerk.ch; ☏ **044/222 19 55**) for exquisitely made upscale Swiss handicrafts; **einzigart** (Josefstrasse 36; www.einzigart.ch; ☏ **044/440 46 00**) for witty yet practical design items, furnishings, and gift ideas; and **Confiserie Sprüngli,** Bahnhofstrasse 21 (see p. 41) for fantastical displays of chocolates and candies.

cabaret voltaire—**BIRTHPLACE OF THE DADA MOVEMENT**

Don't be put off by the somewhat shabby interior of this bar and art gallery—back in 1916, Cabaret Voltaire was the birthplace of the Dada movement. Formed as a "protest against the madness of the times," the venue was frequented by the most avant-garde musicians, thinkers, artists, and literati of the era.

The Dada movement was anti-war, anti-bourgeois, and anarchist in nature, and went on to influence many other genres from surrealism to pop art and punk rock. When World War II came to an end, most Dadaists left Zurich, returning to their home countries. But Cabaret Voltaire lingered on, drawing such painters as Paul Klee and Max Ernst.

Today's "Dadahaus" (as the locals call it) is still patronized by the art-conscious cognoscenti and remains a hip and quirky place for a beer at the heart of the Niederdorf. During the day, the upstairs duDA bar is a place for students to meet for a coffee, or to read or study. By night, the bar is often the venue for art exhibitions, theatrical revues, lectures, and poetry readings. The selection of absinthes here is especially strong. (Spiegelgasse 1; www.cabaretvoltaire. ch; ☏ **043/268 57 20**).

Entertainment & Nightlife

There's more to Swiss entertainment than alphorns and yodeling. Indeed Zurich offers some of Switzerland's best and most sophisticated nightlife, as well as a world-class program of cultural entertainment. Switzerland's finest opera company, the **Zurich Opera,** is located beside the lake in the grandiose neo-baroque **Opernhaus** (Opera House, Falkenstrasse 1; www. opernhaus.ch; ☏ **044/268 66 66**). Placed on the map by such famous composers as Richard Wagner,

Old town Zurich.

Richard Strauss, Paul Hindemith, and Arthur Honegger, it is considered among the world's top opera venues and also an important stage for ballet.

The main classical music venue, the grand **Tonhalle** (Claridenstrasse 7; www.tonhalle-orchester.ch; ✆ **044/206 34 34**), hosts a variety of orchestras and chamber ensembles including its own internationally renowned **Zurich Tonhalle Orchestra.**

The **Schauspielhaus** (Rämistrasse 34; www.schauspielhaus.ch; ✆ **044/258 77 77**) enjoys a reputation as the most prestigious theatre in the German-speaking world, known for its ground-breaking productions of classical and contemporary drama. The Playhouse is situated opposite the Kunsthaus in the city center. It also has a second stage in the avant-garde **Schiffbau** arts complex in Züri West, together with **Moods**, the city's top jazz club (Schiffbaustrasse 4; www.moods.ch; ✆ **044/258 77 77**). The **Widder Bar** (Widder Hotel, Rennweg 7; www.widderhotel.ch; ✆ **044/224 25 26**) is another popular venue for live

Opernhaus, home of Opera Zurich.

The Zurich Street Parade

In recent years, Zurich's Street Parade has overtaken London's Notting Hill Carnival as the largest street festival in the world. Modelled after Berlin's Love Parade, it began in 1992 as a gigantic techno party with just a thousand revelers. Now, with hundreds of DJs; 30-plus floats known as "love mobiles," each with its own dance theme (embracing house, dubstep, trance, techno, and other electronic music styles); and seven fixed stages around the lake, the street parade draws around a million party-goers all in fancy-dress, and the streets are filled with a crazy, hedonistic party atmosphere one Saturday in August. After the official Street Parade, many of the clubs around town host further techno gigs, including the legendary Lethargy party—a 3-day techno dance festival in a converted factory, the **Rote Fabrik** (Seestrasse 395; ✆ **044/485 58 58;** www.rotefabrik.ch; tram 7 [Post Wallishofen]) on the outskirts of the city beside the lake.

jazz during its international concert seasons (autumn and spring).

Advance online booking is highly recommended for most performing arts venues, although you may be lucky and pick up late-release tickets or returns at short notice too.

Zurich has more than 500 **bars and nightspots** catering to all tastes, as well as a flamboyant club scene. In the city center, cool chill-out bars attract an affluent, sophisticated crowd; you'll find some lively beer cellars and many of the gay bars in the Nieder-dorf district, while the newly redeveloped industrial quarter of Züri West boasts a host of ultra-trendy bar and clubs, many housed in former factory buildings.

Our favorite watering-holes include the architecturally striking **Nietturm** (Schiffbaustrasse 4; www.nietturm.ch; ✆ **044/258 77 77**) for stylish cocktails and aerial views of the city in Züri West; the jolly **Zeughauskeller** (see p. 41), the city's top beer hall, in a converted 15th-century arsenal in the city center; the tiny candle-lit subterranean wine bar, **Weinschenke** (Hotel Hirschen; see p. 36) in the Niederdorf for wines from around the world; and trendy **Café Bar Odéon** (Limmatquai 2; www.odeon.ch; ✆ **044/251 16 50;** tram 2, 4, 5, 8, 9, 11, 15 [Bellevue]), an ornate Art Nouveau cafe/bar, once frequented by Lenin, Joyce, Einstein, and Mussolini, and now a popular gay and singles bar by night.

Summer nights are best spent partying in the open-air **Barfuss** bar or chilling with the cool crowd in the riverside bars and open-air cinema zone at **Oberer Letten,** the city's trendiest lido.

Zurich has the highest density of nightclubs in Switzerland, so it's easy to find a place to party late into the night. The city's best-known mainstream nightclub, and still very much the in-place to see and be seen, is **Kaufleuten** (Pelikanstrasse 18; www.kaufleuten.com; ✆ **044/225 33 40;** tram 2, 9 [Sihlstrasse]). Underground dance venue **Zukunft** (Dienerstrasse 33; www.zukunft.cl) is known for its edgy electronic sounds; and **Plaza** (Badenerstrasse 109; www.plaza-zurich.ch; ✆ **044/542 90 90;** tram 2, 3 [Bezirksgebäude]) for high-octane house music and big name DJs. For a grittier nightlife experience, head to the many clubs of Züri West, centered around Escher-Wyss-Platz and Geroldstrasse.

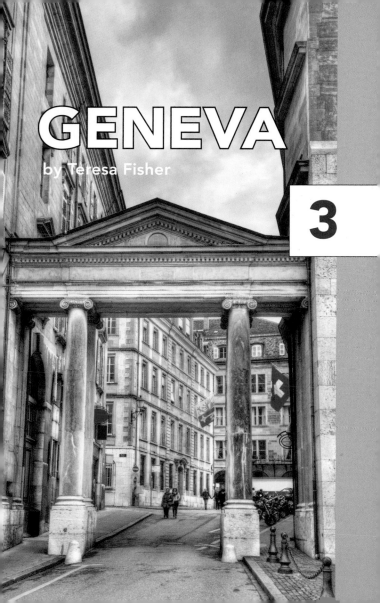

GENEVA

by Teresa Fisher

3

G eneva is Switzerland's second-largest city, and is probably best known for the major role it plays on the world stage, as home to more than 200 major global organizations including the Red Cross and the United Nations.

Consequently, it is the least Swiss of all Swiss cities. Around 40% of its inhabitants are foreigners. It is a cosmopolitan city with a distinctly French flavor and an almost Mediterranean laidback vibe, sitting astride the Franco-Swiss border at the western corner of expansive Lake Geneva (known to the French as Lac Léman), framed by vineyards and overlooked by Europe's tallest mountain, Mont Blanc.

It is also a city of great contrasts, from the narrow cobbled streets and grey-toned severity of the Vieille

PREVIOUS PAGE: **City center of Geneva.**
ABOVE: **A square in Vieille Ville (Old Town), Geneva.**

Ville (Old Town)—which still somehow conveys some of the strict and unyielding morals of what used to be a stronghold of severely punitive Calvinism amid its lively lanes of tiny galleries, boutiques and bistros—to the palatial five-star hotels fringing the vast blue lake, renowned for their extravagance and their fabled Swiss hospitality. The patchwork of parks punctuating the lakeside provide peace and tranquility so rarely found in a city center to the frenetic workings of CERN (the European Center for Nuclear Research), world-leader in particle physics, and the myriad institutions of the International district where, for decades, history has been written.

Elegant and undeniably affluent; dynamic and modern; historic; quirky and characterful—indeed, Geneva radiates a unique atmosphere hard to define although many have tried: "City of Peace," "Smallest of big cities," "Switzerland's international city." The list of ornamental epithets goes on . . .

Essentials

Geneva's tourist office (**Office du Tourisme de Genève**) website is www.geneve-tourisme.ch.

ARRIVING **Geneva International Airport** is situated 4km (2½ miles) northwest of the city center, on the Franco-Swiss border, and can be accessed from both countries. The best way to reach the city center is by train, as taxis are expensive (expect to pay around CHF35 to CHF45 depending on traffic conditions, time of day and number of passengers). By train, it takes just 6 minutes to Geneva-Cornavin (city center). Trains run frequently (every 12 min. in rush hour) from 5:07am to 1:10am, and your transfer from the airport is free: simply take a special UNIRESO ticket from the machine in the baggage collection area of Arrivals and it will entitle you to free public transport in the entire canton of Geneva for a period of up to 80 minutes. This ticket is also valid on any bus: routes 5, 10 and F all operate between the airport and Cornavin station (see below). Some hotels offer a free shuttle bus service.

The main **train station, Gare Cornavin,** has excellent links with European cities. France's high-speed TGV trains from Paris reach Cornavin in just 3 hours (with nine fast trains daily) and there are three express trains to Milan daily (journey time just under four hours). Within Switzerland, it takes 40 minutes to Lausanne (see p. 94), 1 hour to Montreux (see p. 94), less than two hours to Bern, and around three hours to Zurich or Lucerne. Contact **SBB** (**Swiss Federal Railways;** www.sbb.ch; ✆ 0900/300 300) for rail schedules and prices.

If **driving** from Lausanne, head southwest on the A1 along the northern shore of Lake Geneva, to the very far corner of southwestern Switzerland.

There are frequent daily arrivals into Geneva by **lake steamer** year-round from Montreux, Vevey and Lausanne. For the left bank, disembark at the **Jardin Anglais** stop; for the Right Bank you need **Mont Blanc** or **Pâquis.** Contact the **CGN** (Lake Geneva Navigation Company; www.cgn.ch; ✆ 0848/811 848) for further details.

International buses come into Switzerland's largest coach station, the **Gare Routière de Genève** (www.gare-routiere.ch; ✆ 022/732 02 30), near the lake at Place Dorcière. It is also the start-point for sightseeing buses for the city and the region.

CITY LAYOUT It's easy to find your bearings in Geneva, because the city has a relaxed, spread-out feel and is conveniently split into two by the lake and the Rhône River: the **Rive Gauche** (Left or South Bank), which contains the Vieille Ville (Old Town), some major shopping streets, the famous Jet d'Eau (see p. 70) and Floral Clock (see p. 73) and some important museums; and the **Rive Droite** (Right or North Bank), characterized by its grandiose hotels; extensive parks and tree-shaded promenades; and, inland from the lake, some important museums and major international organizations. Within the right and left banks, the city is then further divided into a total of eight official districts (quartiers) and many further neighborhoods, each with its own distinctive character.

GETTING AROUND   Geneva is a sprawling city, and its sights and attractions are quite spread out, especially if you're planning to visit the sights of the International District; or CERN (see p. 75) and Carouge (see p. 73) farther afield. Thankfully, in true Swiss style, the public transport system is ultra-efficient, with buses, trams, and boats to whisk you around town with ease—although you can find traffic

save with the **GENEVA PASS**

Families and avid museum-goers can save by purchasing a Geneva Pass, offering free entry to many top museums and attractions, and free access to the public transport network, plus reductions in some boat trips, tours, shops, and restaurants. The pass is valid for 24, 48, or 72 hours (costing CHF25, CHF35, or CHF45) and is available online in advance at www. geneve-tourisme.ch.

Other savvy travelers plan their visit to Geneva to coincide with the first Sunday of the month, when most museums and galleries are free.

congestion slows up the procedure at times, especially during rush-hour. The best way to explore the bustling web of streets which forms Geneva's hilly historical core, the Old Town, is on foot: The streets are mostly cobbled and public transport limited. It's also especially pleasant to stroll along the quaysides of the lake—to admire its majestic scenery of the city; and the river, to soak up the downtown vibe.

The city's excellent, fully integrated **public transport system** of buses, trams, some trains, and the yellow taxi-boats of the **Mouettes Genevoises** (see below) is operated by **UNIRESO** and **TPG** (**Transports Publics Genevois;** www.tpg.ch; ✆ **0900/022 021**). Services run daily 6am to midnight.

If you're staying in a hotel, youth hostel, or campsite in Geneva, you'll receive a **Geneva Transport Card** free of charge, enabling you to use the entire TPG network of buses, trams, trains, and yellow taxi-boats for free throughout your stay (including the departure day).

Without a Geneva Transport card, expect to pay CHF3/CHF2.50 per adult/child for a single ticket (valid for one hour); CHF2 for a short trip (3 stops by bus/tram or one boat crossing, valid for adults only); or consider getting a 1-day card—at a cost of CHF10.60/CHF7.60 per adult/child, it's often the most cost-effective option. Maps of the transport network, fares and timetables are displayed at all bus and tram stops.

There are many **taxi** companies in Geneva. A taxi can be ordered by phone (call ✆ **022/331 41 33** or ✆ **033/320 22 02**), hailed in the street, or found at taxi stands all over town, at the airport and at the main station, but it's not the most economical or time-efficient way to travel. The minimum fare is CHF6.30, plus a minimum of CHF3.20 per each additional kilometer (CHF3.80 Sundays, evenings, public holidays, and with more than four passengers).

I don't recommend attempting to see Geneva **by car;** parking is difficult and the many one-way streets make navigation complicated.

Cycling is a great way to explore the city, parks, and quays, and ideal if you're planning to venture into the surrounding countryside. From mid-April to mid-October, you can rent bikes from **Genève Roule** for as little as CHF12 a day (CHF8 half-day) or electric bikes from CHF25 a day (CHF17 half-day), from various depots around town, including place de Montbrillant

Events in Geneva

Geneva's calendar is full of festivity year-round, from the fancy-dress parades of February's **Carnival** season, and the world famous **International Motor Show** in March, to the world's largest celebrations outside the USA for **Independence Day;** and the sparkling **Christmas Market,** with its little wooden stalls selling handmade crafts, gingerbread, and mulled wine. But it's most unique event is undoubtedly the historical processions of the **Escalade.**

For centuries, the region of Savoy was a constant threat to Geneva, repeatedly laying siege to the city. One night—11 December

1602—the Genevois victoriously resisted a surprise attack, when the Savoyard troops failed to scale the city walls. Legend has it a housewife, known as the Mère Royaume, tipped a cauldron of scalding vegetable soup over the first soldier's head, then raised the alarm. Ever since, L'Escalade ("The Climbing by Ladder," www.1602. ch) has been celebrated each year, with 3 days and nights of torch-lit costumed processions and festivities, centered on the Old Town. The city's confectioners even sell marmites d'Escalade, chocolate cauldrons filled with marzipan "vegetables."

17 on the right bank, and Ruelle des Templiers 4 on the left bank (www.geneveroule.ch).

No trip to Geneva would be complete without a mini voyage on the lake's **Mouettes Genevoises** (www.mouettesgenevoises.ch; © **022/732 29 44**), the quirky little yellow commuter taxis which ply across the lake from one quayside to the other, carrying businessmen, shoppers, tourists, and all. There are departures roughly every ten minutes from April to October, less frequently in winter months, from Quai du Mont Blanc and Pâquis on the right bank; and from Quai Gustave Ador and Parc des Eaux Vives on the left bank. There is also a crossing every half-hour from Chateaubriand (in Parc Mon Repos) to Port Noir/ Gèneve Plage. The mouettes run from 7:30am until around 9pm weekdays, 10am to 9pm during weekends and public holidays; and you can use the same ticket as for the bus and tram.

The Neighborhoods in Brief

VIEILLE VILLE (OLD TOWN)   The Vieille Ville, on the Rive Gauche or Left Bank, is the historic heart of Geneva and one of its most appealing districts, with its picturesque squares, ornamental fountains, and architectural blends of Gothic, Renaissance and 18th-century features. Built on the tallest hill in town, and topped by the **Cathedral of St Pierre** (see p. 68), its quirky narrow streets are full of bistro-style cafes and locals' bars, fascinating antiques shops, boutiques, and galleries. From here, it is a stone's throw to the cultural hub of Place Neuve, just beyond the old town walls.

RUES BASSES (LOWER TOWN)   Located at the foot of the Vieille Ville on the south bank of the river Rhône (on the Rive Gauche), the Rues Basses literally mean "low streets." These streets form the main commercial and luxury shopping district of Geneva (see **"Shopping,"** p. 90), centered on and around rue du Rhône, rue de la Confédération and rue du Marché. You may also hear locals describe this exclusive shopping area as **Rive.**

THE QUAIS   The lakeside promenades that hug the water's edge around the lake and at the mouth of the River Rhône almost constitute a "neighborhood" of their own. Flanked by grandiose five-star palace hotels and expansive parks, both sides are worth exploring on foot (or aboard one of their mini tourists trains, see p. 75). One of the most scenic walks is from the **Parc des Eaux-Vives** on the Left Bank round to the **Parc de Mon-Repos** on the Right Bank, with impressive views of the city's **Jet d'Eau** (see p. 70) as you go.

PÂQUIS   Once used as a wide-open area for grazing cattle, Pâquis (from the Latin pascuum, meaning "pasture") is a tiny, bustling district brimming with bars and nightclubs, ethnic restaurants, ateliers, hipster boutiques, and curio shops, far removed from the luxurious consumerism of the Rues Basses or the genteel hotels lining the Right Bank just a couple of blocks away. One of Geneva's most animated, down-to-earth districts, it appeals mainly to bargain shoppers and party animals.

INTERNATIONAL DISTRICT   Two kilometers north of the city center, also known as **Pâquis-Nations,** this is a tranquil sector of offices, museums, and neatly manicured parkland. In this district, you'll find the major international organizations, including the impressive European HQ of the United Nations, the World Economic Forum, and the International Red Cross.

Exploring Geneva

It's hard to get lost in Geneva; not only does the lake provide myriad recreational activities and scenic views, but also—together with the River Rhône—it forms a convenient natural boundary between the right and left banks, the Rive Droite and the Rive Gauche.

The atmospheric Vieille Ville (Old Town) at the heart of town (on the Rive Gauche), with its charming old buildings and historical landmarks, its cozy restaurants and tiny boutiques, is tightly compact and popular with everyone; while the world-class museums and galleries, especially those in the European district (on the Rive Droite), enlighten and entertain and serve as living proof of the major role played over the centuries by Geneva, Switzerland's "international" city.

RIVE DROITE

Musée Ariana ★★ MUSEUM This photogenic neoclassical villa—with its domed roof and pastel-pink, heavily ornamented facade, set in gardens overlooking an elegant fountain—is the perfect setting for one of Europe's most important collections of ceramics, and headquarters of the International Academy of Ceramics. It's airy, spacious galleries contain 7 centuries of artifacts (more than 20,000 objects) from the Middle Ages to the present day—and include fine collections of Sévres and Delft, alongside an impressive Islamic collection and some rare treasures from China and Japan. All the main techniques are there: pottery, stoneware, earthenware, porcelain, and china. The museum was built by local arts patron Gustave Revilliod and named after his mother, Ariana de la Rive.

Facade of the Musée Ariana.

The Salon de thé, within the magnificent oval gallery, is a delightful setting to pause for some refreshment. 10 avenue de la Paix. www.ville-ge.ch/ariana. ℭ **022/418 54 50.** Free for permanent collections, CHF8 for temporary exhibitions, free for children under 18. Tues–Sun 10am–6pm.

Musée International de la Croix-rouge et du Croissant-Rouge ★★ MUSEUM   It's hard not to be moved by this heart-rending museum at the headquarters of the International Committee of the Red Cross. It records the history of the Red Cross and Red Crescent organizations, both of which have provided humanitarian aid around the globe since their foundation in Switzerland by Genevese social activist and first Nobel Peace Prize winner Henry Dunant in 1863. He chose the Swiss flag in reverse (a red cross on a white background) as the symbol of the Red Cross movement, easily visible—even in a war zone—and symbolic of neutrality.

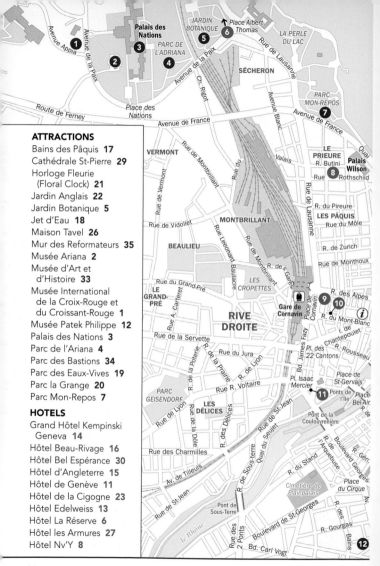

Geneva

```
0        1/4 mi
0     250 m
```

(i) Information

Lac Léman
(Lake Geneva)

Place de
Traînant

FRONTENEX

PARC DES
EAUX-VIVES
19

Quai Gustave Ador

Route de Frontenex

PARC
LA GRANGE
20

Avenue W. Favre

MONTCHOISY

Place de la Navigation

13
13
14
15
16
16

17 17

18
Jet d'Eau

Rade de
Genève

Rue des Eaux-Vives

Rue des Montchoisy

Vollandes

Route de Frontenex

Gare des
Eaux-Vives

Route de Chêne

Av. de l'Amandolier

Rue du
31
Décembre

LES EAUX-VIVES

Sq. du
Mont-
Blanc

Pont du-
Mont-Blanc

JARDIN
ANGLAIS

R. de la Miarie

Av. Pictet De Rochemont

Rue Agasse

Ile
Rousseau

22 21

R. F.Versonnex
Place des
Eaux-Vives

Rue de la Terassière

Pont des
Bergues

Quai Général Guisan

RIVE
GAUCHE

Route de Malagnou

Place du
Rhône

Rue du Rhône

23

rd-pt de Rive
Cours de
Rive

R. Lachenal

RUES
BASSES
24

R. de la
Croix-d'Or

R. de Rive

Rue Hodler

Pl. Em.
Guyenot

R. de la
Confédération

R. du
Marché

27

30

31

Ch. Galland

VIELLE VILLE
(OLD TOWN)
25

26 28
29

32

33

Grand Rue

R. de l'Hôtel-de-Ville

Hôtel de
Ville

Place du
Bourg-de-Four

Bd. Jacques Dalcroze

Helvétique

Bd. des Tranchées

Place
Neuve

R. de la Croix Rouge

35

Rue de l'Athenée

Dufour

PARC DES BASTIONS
Université
34

Cours des Bastions

Rue de l'Athenée

Favon

R. de Candolle

R. St. Léger

Place Ed.
Claparède

Avenue Peschier

PLAINE DE
PLAINPALAIS

Rond-pt. de
Plainpalais Bd. des Philosophes

Av. Henri
Dunant

Bd. de
la Tour

Rue A. Lombard

PARC DES
CHAUMETTES

du Mail

RESTAURANTS

Au Pied de Cochon **31**
Brasserie Lipp **25**
Café de Paris **10**
Chez Ma Cousine **32**
Crêperie St-Pierre **28**
Edelweiss **13**
Globus **24**
La Buvette des Bains **17**
Le Chat Botté **16**
Les Brasseurs **9**

The United Nations of Geneva (UNOG)

The Geneva office of the **United Nations**—the UNOG—has been housed in the Palais des Nations (Palace of Nations) since 1966, as the successor of the now-defunct League of Nations, which was originally set up in 1919 to prevent the recurrence of war on the scale of World War I. The second-largest office of the UN after New York, this immense, mile-long (1.6km) building, set in parkland beside the Musée Ariana (see p. 62), contains more than 4,000 employees and is also the headquarters of numerous international organizations in such fields as peace, human rights, science, and technology, including the World Health Organization and the World Meteorological Organization. Visits are by guided tour only (see below). Remember to bring your passport or you won't be allowed in—as you pass through the gates of UNOG, you are leaving Switzerland and entering international territory!

Its permanent displays are divided into three sections: Defending Human Dignity; Restoring Family Links; and Reducing Natural Risks. Their displays—of rare documents and photography, nonstop film footage, and multimedia displays from the 19th-century battlefields of Europe to the 21st-century plains of Africa—portray just some of the many humanitarian missions carried out by these remarkable organizations in times of war and natural disaster.

17 avenue de la Paix. www.redcrossmuseum.ch. © **022/748 95 25.** Adults CHF15, concessions CHF7, free for children younger than 12. Bus 8, 28, F, V or Z (Appia). Apr–Oct Tues–Sun 10am–6pm, Nov–Mar to 5pm. Closed Mon, Christmas, and New Year.

The Palais des Nations, European headquarters of the United Nations.

Palais des Nations ★★★   You can't fail to spot the brilliantly colored avenue of member flags leading up to the "Palace of Nations," the vast European headquarters of the United Nations. Book in advance to be sure of a place on the fascinating 1-hour guided tours (conducted in any of the UN's official languages), and a chance to set foot in the Assembly Hall, the Court of Honour, and other chambers where international history has been made. Don't miss also the UN's symbolic Armillary Sphere and the Conquest of Space monument in the surrounding gardens, or the massive *Broken Chair* sculpture nearby, by Swiss artist Daniel Berset, a powerful symbol of protest against landmines and cluster bombs.

Parc de l'Ariana, 14 avenue de la Paix. www.unog.ch. ✆ **022/ 917 48 96.** CHF12 (CHF7 for children). Tours daily Mon–Sat, Apr–Aug; Mon–Fri, Sept–Mar (reservations essential; passport required for entry).

RIVE GAUCHE

Cathédrale St-Pierre ★★ CHURCH   A gorgeous fusion of Romanesque, Gothic, and neoclassical styles, St. Peter's Cathedral dominates the Old Town. Built between 1150 and 1232, excavations beneath the edifice have revealed that a Christian sanctuary was sited here as early as A.D. 400 (showcased in the Site Archéologique de Saint-Pierre). The cathedral's austerity dates from the Reformation, when the Genevois gathered in the cloisters in 1536, voted to make St. Peter's Protestant, and stripped all decoration from its once ornate interior. The High Gothic (early 15th-century) Chapelle des Macchabées was used as a storage room during the Reformation. It was restored during World War II. Other highlights of the loft interior include some splendid cross-ribbed vaulting, gigantic rose windows, and an impressive modern organ with 6,000 pipes.

Interior, Cathédrale St-Pierre.

The 145-step climb to the top of the north tower is rewarded by a dramatic bird's-eye view of the city, the lake and beyond—to the Alps to the south, and the Jura Mountains to the north.

Place du Bourg-de-Four 24. www.saintpierre-geneve.ch. ✆ **022/ 311 75 75.** Cathedral: free (donations welcome); tower, CHF4; archaeological site: CHF8. Bus: 36 (Taconnerie). Daily 10am–5pm.

Maison Tavel ★ HISTORIC SITE   Maison Tavel is worth a brief visit because it's the oldest house in Geneva (constructed in 1303 and partially rebuilt after a fire in 1334) and it's also home to the **Museum of Ancient Geneva.** The house has undergone several transformations over the centuries, but it retains many traditional elements, including an attractive courtyard, staircase, cellar, and back garden. The museum contains a fascinating albeit small collection of antique furniture, tapestries and silverware, illustrating Genevois lifestyle from the medieval times to the late 19th-century, and don't miss the fascinating model of 19th-century Geneva on the third floor . . . How times have changed!

6, rue du Puits Saint-Pierre. www.ville-ge.ch. ✆ **022/418 37 00.** Free admission to permanent collection, 5F temporary expositions. Bus: 36 (Hôtel de Ville). Tues–Sun 10am–6pm.

Musée d'Art et d'Histoire ★★ MUSEUM   The 100-year-old galleries of Geneva's premier museum are a veritable treasure trove with nearly a million *objets d'art* spanning the centuries. It is an eclectic collection, with something to please everyone: The Archaeology wing houses relics from ancient Egypt, Greece and Rome; the Fine Arts wing contains paintings from the Renaissance to the 20th century; there's medieval furniture, weaponry, stained glass, timepieces, musical instruments, and more in the Applied Arts wing. Don't try to see everything. Art lovers make a beeline for the Impressionist collection, with works by Chagall, Monet, Picasso, Renoir, Rodin, and van Gogh.

rue Charles-Galland 2. www.ville-ge.ch/mah. ℂ **022/418 26 00.** Free; temporary exhibitions CHF5–CHF20. Bus: 1, 8 (Tranchées); Bus: 3, 5, 7, 36 (Athenée). Tues–Sun 11am–6pm.

Musée Patek Philippe ★★ MUSEUM The world's most extensive and prestigious watch collection is housed in an extravagant museum belonging to the renowned local timepiece-makers and one of the city's most venerated companies, Patek Philippe. Geneva has led the world in watchmaking ever since austere Calvinist times, and on the ground floor, you can see more than 200 machines and tools used by watchmakers, engravers, and goldsmiths over the centuries. The second floor contains the Patek Philippe Collection, and the fourth floor hosts a small but fascinating display devoted to the measurement of time throughout the ages. Devote the majority of your time to the third floor, with its spectacular array of 16th- to 19th-century European and Swiss watches: Star

THE jet d'eau

Geneva's best-known landmark, the Water Jet or **Jet d'Eau** ★★★ (known affectionately to the Genevois as the *jeddo*), never fails to turn heads as it spurts a staggering 500 liters (132 gallons) of water per second—that's around five bathtubs of water—140m (460 ft.) into the air above the lake. This jet was originally a pressure release for a hydro-powered factory, but the locals liked it so much that in 1891 they converted it into a fountain.

A rainbow reflected in the Jet d'Eau.

attractions here include the 17th-century astronomical watch and a charming collection of bejeweled animal-shaped timepieces. And don't miss the museum's pride and glory, the Calibre 89, the most complicated watch ever made.

rue des Vieux Grenadiers 7. www.patekmuseum.com. ℰ **022/ 807 09 10.** Adults CHF10, free for children under 18. Bus. 1 (École-de-Médicine); Tram: 12 (Plainpalais). Tues–Fri 2pm– 6pm, Sat 10am–6pm.

Parks & Gardens

It may be Switzerland's second city, but Geneva is amazingly green nonetheless. Take a pleasant stroll along the quays of the Rive Droite, past the vibrant **Bains des Pâquis lido ★★★,** located on a promontory jutting into the lake, where weather permitting you can take a quick dip, chill on the beach, or drink in views of snow-clad Mount Blanc over a coffee en route. Beyond the lido, you'll arrive at some of the lushest parks in Geneva.

The Horloge Fleurie (Floral Clock) at Jardin Anglais.

There's tranquil **Parc Mon-Repos ★★** with its first-rate restaurant, **La Perle du Lac ★★** (126 rue de Lausanne; www.laperledulac.ch; ✆ **022/909 10 20**), popular with the well-heeled of Geneva and the local business community for its classic French cuisine, its local fish dishes, and its exemplary list of Swiss wines. Just beyond, Mediterranean blooms, giant cacti, and pink flamingos vie for attention at the luscious lakeside **Jardin Botanique ★★**, while nearby **Parc de l'Ariana ★** shelters **Musée Ariana ★★** (see p. 62) and the iconic United Nations building, the **Palais des Nations ★★★** (see p. 67).

Catch a boat to the other side of the lake and get off at quai Gustave-Ador on the Rive Gauche. From here you can explore two more lakeside parks, **Parc des Eaux-Vives ★,** Geneva's oldest park; and neighboring **Parc la Grange ★,** which boasts the Confederation's most extravagant rose garden.

Behind the Vieille Ville, locals congregate to play chess on giant boards in the shady **Parc des Bastions ★,** alongside the **Mur des Reformateurs ★★,**

Mur des Reformateurs.

a massive wall of bas-reliefs commemorating Jean Calvin and other key figures of the Reformation.

Downtown, between the main shopping district and the lake, the **Jardin Anglais** ★ contains one of the city's biggest tourist draws—the **Horloge Fleurie (Floral Clock)** ★★. Created from 6,500 flowers, and always ticking, it celebrates the Swiss tradition of watch- and clock-making.

Outlying Attractions

If time permits, the outskirts of Geneva are well worth exploring, in particular the characterful suburb of **Carouge** (just 15 min. from the city center by tram 12 or 13 to Marché) across the L'Arve River on the southwest perimeter of Geneva. Annexed in the 18th century to the Kingdom of Sardinia, this tiny, residential district has a distinctly Mediterranean, village-like feel. You're sure to be captivated by its sunny squares and its attractive Italianate architecture, not to mention its

Carouge square.

bohemian sidewalk cafes, jazz clubs, artisan markets, and kooky boutiques. It also boasts some top-notch restaurants, including **A L'Olivier de Provence ★★** (rue Jacques-Dalphin 13; www.olivier-de-provence.ch; ✆ **022/342 04 50**) and the more modestly priced **Café des Négociants ★** (rue de la Filature 29; www.negociants.ch; ✆ **022/300 31 30**).

Another excursion, and an absolute must for foodies, is a visit to the **Domaine de Châteauvieux ★★★** (16 Chemin de Châteauvieux, Peney-Dessus; www.chateauvieux.ch; ✆ **022/753 15 11**), a 16th-century luxury country-house hotel and restaurant northwest of the city center at **Peney-Dessus.** This is Geneva's top eatery, thanks to Swiss chef/owner Philippe Chevrier, who uses the finest of seasonal produce from the property's vegetable gardens and vines to create his two-Michelin-starred haute cuisine. Stay the night and even breakfast is a treat, especially in the summer, when it is served alfresco on the floral-filled veranda.

Organized Tours & Excursions

A number of companies offer city tours and various transport modes. For the most scenic vistas, go by boat.

Compagnie Générale de Navigation (CGN) offers a popular hour-long lake cruise (with several departures daily May–Sept) enabling you to see some of key sights of Geneva as well as the beautiful countryside and châteaux bordering the lake beyond the city limits (www.cgn.ch; ✆ **0848/811 848;** 8 quai du Mont-Blanc). **Swiss Boat** offers similar hour-long cruises of the city quaysides but on smaller vessels; plus a 2¾-hour Rhône River tour (www.swissboat.com; ✆ **022/732 47 47;** 4 quai du Mont-Blanc).

On dry land, I like the **STT Trains** tours, especially if you have kids in tow: just hop aboard one of their open-sided mini tourist trains and explore the city (with recorded multilingual commentary) on one of three circuits: the Old Town (35 min., CHF11); the International Tour (exploring the buildings of the UN and other international organizations plus the left bank, 90 min., CHF25); or Parks and Residences, along the

CERN—the European Center for Nuclear Research

A visit to CERN is a truly a mind-boggling experience, even for scientists. The world-renowned European Center for Nuclear Research (CERN; Route de Meyrin 385, Meyrin; www.cern.c/expoglobe; ✆ **022/767 76 76;** free admission) was built in 1954 near Geneva to analyze the fundamental laws of nature. The Large Hadron Collider is the latest experiment, started in 2010 and comprising a 17-mile-long (27-km) underground accelerator tunnel—the most complex electronic equipment ever built. It recreates the conditions less than a billionth of a second after the Big Bang, helping to explain the origins and structure of the universe. The World Wide Web was developed in CERN in 1990, and you can visit the hands-on Microcosm Museum and the unique Universe of Particles exhibition here to discover more.

right bank (35 min., CHF9). Trains depart at 45-minute intervals from quai du Mont-Blanc (or place du Rhône for the Old Town tour) daily from April to October; weekends only in March, November, and December. You can find further information at www.trains-tours.ch; ✆ **022/781 04 04.**

Explore the Vieille Ville on foot on a 2-hour guided **walking tour** every Saturday at 10am starting at the Tourist Office at Rue du Mont-Blanc 18 (www.geneve-tourisme.ch); or on Segway with **Citywheels,** daily at 10am and 2pm starting at Citywheels' offices beside Cornavin railway station (rue de Lausanne 16-20; www.citywheels.ch; ✆ **022/510 34 56;** 1½ hours; CHF99; minimum age 16, driving license required). If you fancy a Segway tour, but are concerned about negotiating the cobbled streets of the old town, they also offer a 2½-hour Segway tour of the International Quarter and surrounding parkland for CHF129.

There are also some excellent **biking** excursions: Choose from a variety of themes and distances including "Science and Nature," a "Wine Tour," "Famous painters in Geneva," and "Chocolate tasting and famous love letters." Contact **eBike Tour** (www.ebike tour.ch; ✆ **079/623 50 56**) to get the lowdown.

Where to Stay

As a truly world-class city, it will come as no surprise that Geneva has numerous top-notch hotels to match. But be forewarned—the city frequently hosts a number of international conferences and conventions, so many of its hotels are booked months in advance. And while it does incorporate dozens of expensive hotels in all different architectural styles (from the antique to the super modern), it lacks intimate, family-run inns.

The more affordable accommodation—and none of it is cheap—tends to be inland from the lake, clustered around the railway terminal, or on the Rive Gauche. The palatial lakeside hotels which stretch along the Rive Droite count among the nation's top addresses; their fabled Swiss hospitality (which in Geneva comes at times with a particularly high price-tag) is second-to-none.

ON THE RIVE DROITE
Expensive
Grand Hôtel Kempinski Geneva ★ Don't be put off by the ugly concrete facade of the Kempinsky Geneva. Inside, this sleek, modern hotel offers space, elegance, comfort, and unrivalled views from its waterfront position on the western shore of the lake, just 15 minutes from the airport and 5 minutes from the main financial sector of central Geneva. Expect bright, spacious bedrooms overlooking the lake, decorated in soft, warm hues, with contemporary fittings and marble bathrooms. It is also an excellent, albeit pricey, choice for families: The Kempinski Kids Club provides childcare for children ages 3 to 8, and the hotel boasts the largest private indoor swimming pool in the city.

Quai du Mont-Blanc 19. www.kempinski geneva.com. ☏ **022/ 908 90 81.** 398 units. Doubles from CHF460, suites from CHF5,000. Bus: 1, 25 (Monthoux). **Amenities:** 3 restaurants; bar; gym; spa; saltwater swimming pool; shopping arcade; business facilities; babysitting; concierge; chauffeur service; Kids' Club (ages 3–8); free Wi-Fi.

Hôtel Beau-Rivage ★★ Hotel Beau-Rivage is the oldest hotel in Geneva, operating since 1865 here on the waterfront and still managed by the fifth generation of the founding Mayer family. Its star-studded guest list

A suite at the Hotel Beau Rivage.

has included such luminaries as Sarah Bernhardt, the Duke and Duchess of Windsor, and, more recently, Sting and Catherine Deneuve. The hotel also has an illustrious, sometimes-violent, history: Empress Elisabeth of Austria was stabbed near here in 1898 by anarchist Luigi Lucheni, and the birth of Czechoslovakia as an independent nation was signed here in 1918. Today, the Beau-Rivage provides its guests with 21st-century amenities and impeccable service, while retaining a rarified atmosphere that's evident from the moment you step into the elegant five-story open lobby, or into the suites with their wood paneling and Italian frescoes. There's a certain air of decadence here—it feels a bit like staying in a stately home. The rooms are all beautifully decorated with opulent fabrics and antique furnishings. The hotel's Michelin-starred restaurant, **Le Chat-Botté** ★★★ (see p. 83), counts among the top eateries in town.

Quai du Mont-Blanc 13. www.beau-rivage.ch. ☏ **022/716 66 66.** 168 units. Doubles from CHF870, suites from CHF1,620.

Bus: 1 (Monthoux). **Amenities:** 2 restaurants; bar; babysitting; concierge; chauffeur; gym; room service; free Wi-Fi.

Hôtel d'Angleterre ★★★   Situated on the lakeshore, the palatial Hôtel d'Angleterre is the smaller, more affordable neighbor of the celebrated Beau Rivage (see above) and one of the city's most pleasing hotels. Despite the antiquated lift, this elegant hotel is run to perfecting standards and, as the name implies, the rooms are tastefully outfitted in a style reminiscent of an extravagant English country house, with sumptuous fabrics and fittings and soothing lighting. Most rooms have lake views (the smaller rooms have lake glimpses) and the suites are especially plush, with spacious marble bathrooms. Service is exemplary; the concierge is especially accommodating, and I love the quirky Leopard Room bar, with its safari-inspired decor and extensive whisky selection.

17 Quai de Mont-Blanc. www.dangleterrehotel.com. © 022/906 55 55. 45 units. Doubles CHF790–1100, suites CHF1,800–6,900. Bus: 1, 25 (Monthoux). **Amenities:** Restaurant; bar; concierge; pet; gym; sauna; limousine service; free Wi-Fi.

Hôtel La Réserve ★★★   This contemporary five-star hotel is set in 10 acres of gardens beside the lake on the outskirts of town, with decadent, stylish interiors by maverick Parisian designer Jacques Garcia. Taking inspiration from the style of African lodges, each room offers the ultimate in comfort, with crisp white cotton, velvet, and linen bed-clothing; sleek mosaic and granite bathrooms; and a terrace overlooking the gardens and lake. But La Réserve's real draw is its world-renowned spa. Best-known for its iconic 4- or 7-day Nescens "better-aging" programs (which help you to preserve your youthfulness by analyzing all aspects of your body, lifestyle, and diet), the spa also offers acupuncture, osteopathy, aesthetic angiology for the face and legs, Shiatsu, and reflexology. There's also a swimming pool, tennis courts, endless treatment rooms, and an organic restaurant. For children, there's "La Petite Reserve" club—a supervised play area and parent-free zone—for ages 6 months to 13 years, and a summer camp that offers weeklong multi-sport courses for 6- to 11-year-olds.

301 Route de Lausanne. www.lareserve.ch. ☎ **022/959 59 99.** 102 units. Doubles CHF600–CHF3,100. Train: Tuilleries, then 2-minutes' walk. **Amenities:** Spa; swimming pool; 5 restaurants; bar; DJ; kids' club; tennis courts; gardens; water taxi to city center; free Wi-Fi.

Moderate

Hôtel N'vY ★   This hotel near exudes boho chic, with its flamboyant bars and cafe open round the clock. The minimalist rooms boast state-of-the-art furnishings, with sharp, clean lines in a variety of vibrant colors and textures. The hotel's see-and-be-seen venues include the fashionable Trilby Restaurant with its arty fusion cuisine, the ultra-sophisticated cocktail bar NVY (with a resident DJ daily 6pm–1am), and cozy Tag's Cafe, which provides iPads for its guests. The price tag for all of this is surprisingly affordable—stay here and you'll be the "envy" of all your friends.

55 rue Rothschild. www.hotelnvygeneva.com. ☎ **022/544 66 66.** 153 units. Doubles from CHF184. Tram: 15 (Butini). **Amenities:** Restaurant; cafe; bar; gym; DJ; free Wi-Fi.

Inexpensive

Hôtel de Genève ★   This cheap and cheerful, two-star Belle Époque hotel appeals to budget travelers who don't mind a no-frills atmosphere if it means saving on room costs. The rooms are very basic but spotlessly clean, the bathrooms tiny but adequate. The decor is generally quite quirky, with an abundance of fairy-lights and florid ornaments in public areas, but I especially like the cozy Alpine-chalet atmosphere of the main reception area. The staff is friendly and the buffet breakfasts—with their cold cuts, cereals, and pastries—are big, tasty, and filling. Take note if you need quiet to sleep: Some of the rooms are quite noisy due to the hotel's proximity to the train station.

1 place Isaac-Mercier. www.hotel-de-geneve.ch. ✆ **022/908 54 00.** 39 units. Singles from CHF104, doubles from CHF135. Bus: 10 (Place des 22 Cantons); Tram: 15, 16 (Isaac-Mercier). **Amenities:** Bar; cafeteria/coffee shop; free Internet in lobby.

Hôtel Edelweiss ★★   Don't be fooled by the modern facade of Hôtel Edelweiss—it's the perfect retreat if you haven't time to stay in the Swiss countryside. Step inside, away from the bustling streets of the lively Pâquis district, and you'll be transported straight to the mountains. Friendly staff dressed in traditional costumes; log fires; fresh flowers; and snug, wood-clad guest rooms with plush fabrics in earthy hues and rustic hand-painted furniture combine to create the atmosphere of an authentic alpine hotel. Book well in advance to clinch one of the roomy family rooms. I love the quirky eponymous restaurant in the basement (**Edelweiss ★★;** see p. 85), which serves a simple menu of Swiss specialties, including some of the best fondues in town.

2 place de la Navigation. www.hoteledelweissgeneva.com. ✆ **022/544 51 51.** 42 units. Doubles from CHF138. Tram: 13, 14 (Place de la Navigation); Bus: 1 (Place de la Navigation). **Amenities:** Restaurant; free Wi-Fi.

ON THE RIVE GAUCHE
Moderate
Hôtel de la Cigogne ★★★   It's easy to spot the Hôtel de la Cigogne, with its smart orange awnings

and ornamental gold stork, La Cigogne, above the entrance. Once inside, the ornate interiors instantly conjure up a sense of comforting luxury. Each room is elegant, spacious and refined, exquisitely decorated with antiques from an assortment of periods and styles, and featuring luxurious marble bathrooms. Service is top-notch, and fresh flowers and log fires add the finishing touches to this homey hotel located just off the lakeside and at the foot of the Old Town.

17 place Longemalle. www.cigogne.ch. ☏ **022/818 40 40.** 52 units. Doubles CHF485–CHF620, suites CHF615–CHF2,050. Bus: 6, 8, 9 (Metropole). **Amenities:** Restaurant; concierge, room service; free Wi-Fi.

Hôtel les Armures ★★★   Hôtel les Armures is an intimate and historic hotel, located at the top of the Old Town, which was converted from four buildings dating from the 13th to 17th centuries. The guest rooms blend modern furnishings with original decorative details, such as painted ceilings, frescoes, wood beams, exposed stonework, and open fireplaces. For the best view, request a room overlooking the quiet, shaded square with its ancient fountain. You may find yourself rubbing shoulders with celebrities here: The hotel's guest list has included luminaries such as Queen Sofia of Spain, Sofia Loren, Paul McCartney, Monica Seles, and George Clooney. There's even a plaque near the front door commemorating Bill and Hillary Rodham Clinton's visit in 1994. And if you're hungry, you won't have to go far: The hotel's eponymous restaurant—a cozy wood-beamed eatery adorned with muskets and armor—is a veritable fondue institution.

1 rue Puits-St Pierre. www.hotel-les-armures.ch. ☏ **022/310 91 72.** 32 units. Doubles from CHF430. Bus: 36 (Cathédrale); Tram: 12 (Rive or Molard). **Amenities:** Restaurant; bar; concierge; room service; babysitting; limousine service; free Wi-Fi.

Inexpensive

Hôtel Bel Espérance ★★   On the slopes at the entrance to the Old Town, just a stone's throw from some of the city's most luxurious shopping boulevards, this unpretentious budget hotel is owned and managed by the Salvation Army. Expect simple, functional rooms (including some generously sized family rooms)—not dissimilar to an upmarket hostel—private bathrooms, and fantastic views across the rooftops to the lake.

1 rue de la Vallée. www.hotel-bel-esperance.ch. ✆ **022/818 37 37.** 40 units. Doubles CHF160–CHF190, family rooms CHF235. Bus: 10, 33, A, E, G (Rive). **Amenities:** Kitchen; terrace; laundry room; free Wi-Fi.

Where to Eat

Thanks to the strong international flavor of the city, eating out in Geneva is a cosmopolitan experience, with restaurants serving food from around the world. Given their proximity to the French border, the Swiss cuisine here has an unmistakably French influence, with cozy Paris-style bistros alongside the plentiful fine-dining options. Meals are often long, drawn-out affairs and, in most cases, more expensive than many travelers are used to. Local delicacies include filets of perch or omble chevalier from the lake; and the local longeole sausage; and traditional Swiss cheese dishes such as fondue and raclette, ideally accompanied by local Geneva wines.

ON THE RIVE DROITE

Expensive

Le Chat-Botté ★★★ FRENCH   Situated in the five-star **Hôtel Beau-Rivage ★★** (see p. 77), Le Chat-Botté ("Puss in Boots") is a classical-style restaurant serving some of the finest food in town, and is popular for both pleasurable business lunches and romantic treats, especially during the summer months, when you can dine on the beautiful terrace with a sweeping panorama of the lake. In the capable hands of French Michelin-starred chef Dominique Gauthier, you will be assured of exemplary French cuisine cooked with ingredients sourced from the finest producers, including foie gras from the Landes, snails from Vallorbes, and suckling lamb from the Pyrenees—plus a host of delectable *amuse-bouches* to tickle your taste buds, and some exceptional French wines. Choose from the four-course set menus for the best value—the earth menu, the sea menu, or, for that special occasion, the prestigious (and expensive) set menu that's served to the entire table. Reservations are strongly advised.

Hôtel Beau-Rivage, Quai du Mont-Blanc 13. www.beau-rivage. ch. ☏ **022/716 69 39.** Mains CHF60–CHF105, set 3-course lunch menu CHF70, dinner menus from CHF140. Bus: 1, 25 (Monthoux); Bus: 6, 8, 9, 25, 61 (Mont Blanc). Mon–Fri noon– 1:45pm (last order), 7pm–9:45pm (last order); Sat 7–9:45pm (last order).

Moderate

Brasserie Lipp ★ SEAFOOD/FRENCH You could be forgiven for thinking you were in the French capital when you visit this stylish restaurant (located on the second floor of a chic shopping mall and named after the renowned Parisian brasserie), with its waiters in black jackets and long white aprons, and a typical old-world brasserie ambience. Fresh oysters are a specialty, and so is fresh lobster, which diners can choose from a tank. Other signature dishes include regional favorites from southwest France, such as charcuterie and *cassoulet*—a flavorful sausage and white bean casserole, slow-cooked the traditional way in a deep earthenware dish. The enormous freshest-of-fresh shellfish platters are not for the faint-hearted; however, they are as every bit as delicious as they are spectacular. Lipp is an especially popular venue for business entertaining, so booking is advisable, even at lunchtime.

Rue de la Confédération 8. www.brasserie-lipp.com. ℂ **022/ 318 80 30.** Mains CHF23–CHF50, plat du jour CHF19–CHF37. Bus: 1, 2, 3, 5, 7, 9, 10, 19, 20, 29; Tram: 12, 16, 17 (Bel-Air). Mon–Sat 7am–2am, Sun 9am–2am.

Café de Paris ★★★ FRENCH   This lavishly decorated bistro, dubbed "Chez Boubier" by its devoted local clientele, conjures up an atmosphere reminiscent of the Parisian brasseries of the 1930s with its simple wooden tables, wooden wall panels, chandeliers, and its brisk, efficient service. However, it's definitely one to miss if you're vegetarian as it only serves one main course—premium *entrecôte* steak, cooked to perfection to your specifications and served dripping with herb butter (invented here by Monsieur Boubier in the 1930s), three helpings of fries, and a generous, tastily dressed green salad. There's a choice of sorbets, ice cream, fruit salad, or patisseries for dessert. The whole experience is simple but delicious.

Rue du Mont-Blanc 26. www.chezboubier.com. ℂ **022/732 84 50.** Mains from CHF42. Train: Cornavin. Daily 7am–11pm.

Edelweiss ★★ SWISS   Extremely touristy, and especially popular with families, this basement restaurant serves hearty Swiss cuisine in a witty setting reminiscent of a mountain chalet: think red-and-white-checked tablecloths; alphorns, edelweiss, toy St. Bernard dogs, and other kitsch local memorabilia adorning the wood-paneled walls; and an oom-pah band and occasional yodeler in its midst. The fondues (from CHF28 per person) are scrumptious, plus there are plenty of other authentic Swiss specialties for non-cheese-lovers, including rösti potatoes; filets of perch from the lake; and *fondue bourguignonne* (beef fondue served with frites and sauces), all washed down with local wines.

Hôtel Edelweiss, Place de la Navigation (off rue de Berne). www.hoteledelweissgeneva.com. ℂ **022/544 51 51.** Mains: CHF20–CHF54, 3-course menus from CHF48. Tram: 13, 14 (Place de la Navigation); Bus: 1 (Place de la Navigation). 7pm–11pm daily.

Globus ★★ INTERNATIONAL   From breakfast through lunch and dinner to late-night snack, it's fun to eat and drink your way around the world in the massive, modernistic food hall of Globus, Geneva's upscale department store at the heart of a chic shopping neighborhood. Choose from tapas, panini, noodles, crêpes, curries, sushi, salads, caviar, seafood—you name it, they have it here, from light bites to more substantial meals. The fare is essentially high-quality fast food (with a rather elevated price tag), prepared on the spot and served at individual shiny black-and-chrome bars. There are plenty of desserts too, including cakes and pastries, and a wellness bar that serves freshly squeezed juices and smoothies. Even the wine bar offers a choice of wines from around the globe. Unsurprisingly popular with well-heeled shoppers looking for a quick, quality lunch, the whole informal, self-service eating experience makes a pleasant change from the more conventional (and time-consuming) sit-down restaurant.

48 rue du Rhône. www.globus.ch. ℂ **058/578 50 50.** Mains from CHF20. Tram: 16 (Molard). Mon–Fri 7:30am–10pm, Sat 8:30am–10pm.

Inexpensive

La Buvette des Bains ★ INTERNATIONAL   On first impression, the unprepossessing exterior of this somewhat shabby, ramshackle, whitewashed hut— located on a pier in the middle of Lake Geneva—seems an unlikely venue for an lively cafe/bar; a place where locals meet for coffee and cake; simple soups and salads; platters of cold cuts; a wholesome *plat du jour;* or simply just a drink. But perhaps it's best known for its top-notch breakfasts (served 8–11:30am)—the traditionally Swiss Bircher Muesli is especially delicious— and on winter evenings (Sept–Apr), its superb cheese fondues. The shack is located at the far end of the Bains de Pâquis, and is accessed by means of a long wooden boardwalk over the lake. Hugely popular year-round, it draws a young, trendy crowd (huddled round wood stoves in winter, and basking on the terraces in summer), and with families who flock to the beaches and lido-style swimming area in sunny weather. Cash only.

Bains de Pâquis, 30 quai du Mont-Blanc. www.buvettedes bains.ch. © **022/738 16 16.** Plat du jour CHF14. Bus: 1 (Pâquis). 7am-10:30pm daily.

Les Brasseurs ★★ ALSATIAN   Centrally located by Cornavin train station, this jolly restaurant draws a young, lively crowd for its menu of tasty German and Alsatian specialties. It's also the only venue in Geneva that brews its own *blanche, blonde,* and *ambrée* beers. These ales provide the perfect accompaniment to the hearty, wholesome cuisine, and you can buy them (or a souvenir glass) to take away—they are sold by the bottle or the barrel. Our favorites here are the thin, crisp *flammeküches,* the Alsatian equivalent of a pizza, made with various toppings that include bacon, onion, cream, cheese, tomatoes, mushrooms, and olives. The salads are generous, and the *choucroute* (braised sauerkraut and sausage) and *carbonnade de boeuf* (a rich beef stew)—both cooked in Les Brasseurs' beer—are standouts. Make a reservation or arrive before 9pm to be sure of a table.

Place de Cornavin 20. www.les-brasseurs.ch. ℭ **022/731 02 06.** Main dishes CHF16–CHF31, plat du jour CHF17–CHF19. Train: Cornavin. Mon–Wed 11am–1am (2am Thurs–Sat), Sun 3pm–1am.

ON THE RIVE GAUCHE
Moderate
Au Pied de Cochon ★★ FRENCH/SWISS   Centrally located at the heart of the Old Town, on the lane that leads downhill from the picturesque Place du Bourg-de-Four, Au Pied de Cochon is very much a Genevois institution that appeals to locals as well as tourists for its high-quality, hearty, traditional fare. The setting is classic turn-of-the-century brasserie, with wood paneling, leather banquettes, white linen tablecloths, and mirrors; the first-class service is brisk and efficient. The main draw on the menu, as the name suggests, is a stuffed pig's trotter served with Madeira sauce and market vegetables. But for those with more conservative tastes, the risotto with pan-fried duck liver and local Swiss sausage, or the traditional beef stew are equally delectable. The wine list has a choice of French and Swiss wines, served by the glass or the bottle, with a notable selection of excellent wines from the Geneva region.

4 Place du Bourg-de-Four. www.pied-de-cochon.ch. ℭ **022/ 310 47 97.** Mains CHF29–CHF65, plat du Jour CHF20. Bus: 3, 5 (Croix-Rouge), 36 (Bourg-de-Four). Mon–Fri 8am–midnight, Sat–Sun 11am–midnight.

Inexpensive

Chez Ma Cousine ★★★ SWISS Visit Chez Ma Cousine for delicious Swiss-style fast food. In a happening location at the heart of the Old Town, this cheery, bright-yellow restaurant offers a great value, making it exceptionally family-friendly and popular with students. No airs and graces here, just good-quality, simple home cooking. The full name is actually "Chez Ma Cousine on y Mange du Poulet" ("At my cousin's house we eat chicken") and accordingly, there's only one dish on the menu: Grilled chicken, served with mountains of crispy sautéed Provençale-style potatoes and a salad, followed by a choice of simple, tempting desserts, such as chocolate mousse or *tarte tatin*. Wines are served by the glass or by the bottle. Service is speedy, so the restaurant doesn't take reservations.

Place du Bourg de Four 6. www.chezmacousine.ch. © **022/310 96 96.** Mains CHF15. Bus: 36 (Bourg-de-Four). Mon–Sat 11am–11:30pm, Sun 11am–12:30pm.

Crêperie St-Pierre ★★ FRENCH Crêperie St-Pierre, in the heart of Old Town, is the perfect place to tuck into authentic Breton crêpes, washed down the traditional way with cider, or with wine by the glass. This cozy but no-frills cafe crammed full of tiny tables serves an impressive choice of tasty, affordable pancakes (both sweet and savory) plus copious salads. The food is simple, without garnish, but nourishing and a good value for the money/location. I really like the crêpe sarrasin (made with buckwheat) laden with juicy strips of steak and onion, followed by a sweet pancake with sugar, cinnamon and butter—simple but delicious. Warning: Only order a second pancake if you're seriously hungry! In summer, the cobbled pavement terrace is an especially pleasant spot for lunch, in a sunny pedestrian corner right beside the cathedral. The clientele here consists primarily of tourists (plus an occasional smattering of regular locals), and service can be slow and quality variable, especially during high season.

6 Place de la Taconnerie. © **022/310 09 76.** CHF8–CHF20. Bus: 36 (Taconnerie). Daily noon–10pm.

Shopping

From boutiques to department stores, Geneva is a shopper's dream come true. The city is world-renowned for its watches and jewelry, but it's also a good place to buy embroidered blouses, music boxes from the Jura region, chocolate, Swiss Army knives, and many other items.

Geneva practically invented the wristwatch. In fact, watchmaking in the city dates from the 16th century. Here, more than in any other Swiss city, you should be able to find all the best brands, including Philippe Patek, Tissot, Rolex, Omega, and Blancpain, to name just a few. Be careful not to buy a Swiss watch in one of the souvenir stores; if jewelers are legitimate, they'll display the symbol of the Geneva Association of Watchmakers and Jewelers. **Bucherer,** 45 rue du Rhône (www.bucherer.com; © **022/319 62 66**), one of the nation's leading watch and jewelry retailers, always has a plentiful selection.

An ideal place to start your shopping spree is upscale **place du Molard** on the left bank, and its flanking streets—rue du Rhône and rue du Marché—ogle at the dazzling jewelry, the luxury brands, and the latest in haute couture Genevois, but try not to look at the price tags. Here too are chic department stores

Globus, 48 rue du Rhône (www.globus.ch; ☏ **058/ 578 50 50**) and **Bon Genie,** 34 rue du Marché (www.bongenie-grieder.ch; ☏ **022/818 11 11**). Just around the corner, stock up on picnic supplies at **Halle-de-Rive,** 29 boulevard Helvétique (www.halle-de-rive.com), an exclusive indoor market with fine cheeses, cold cuts, bread, fruit, and vegetables.

The cobbled streets of the Old Town contain the quirkier boutiques and fine arts, while bohemian **Carouge** is the place to seek out more whimsical arts and crafts, antiquities, and local designs. There's a charming **Farmers' Market** in Place du Marché on Wednesday and Saturday mornings.

Some of the world's most famous auction houses are also located in the city, including **Sotheby's,** 13 quai du Mont-Blanc; **Christie's,** 8 place de la Taconnerie; and **Antiquorum,** 2 rue du Mont-Blanc, the largest repository of antique timepieces in the world. The tourist office has details of forthcoming sales.

Entertainment & Nightlife

The grand 19th-century opera house, the **Grand Théâtre ★★★,** has earned international repute for its world-class opera, theatre, ballet, classical concerts, and chamber recitals. Modelled on Paris's acclaimed Opera Garnier, the Grand Théâtre seats 1,500 and is the largest theatre in French-speaking Switzerland. The main opera and ballet season spans September through July, with an ambitious program from its resident companies, as well as performances from such guest troupes as Lausanne's world-renowned Béjart dance troupe.

Also in Place Neuve, Geneva's acclaimed **Orchestre de la Suisse Romande** performs regular classical concerts in the rococo-style **Victoria Hall** ★★, the city's main musical institution.

Don't be fooled by the city's seemingly stately veneer, as Geneva has a surprisingly diverse and varied after-dark scene, which starts to warm up as the sun goes down and neon lights begin to illuminate the lake. In summer, the **outdoor cafes and bars** lining the banks of the river and the lake are always a good starting point for an evening out. You'll find other popular watering holes in and around **place du Bourg-de-Four**—once a 19th-century stagecoach stop, this pebbled square is now one of the nightlife hubs of Geneva's Old Town.

For a listing of nightlife and cultural activities, pick up a copy of the free bilingual monthly *Genève Le Guide* (www.le-guide.ch) from your hotel or tourist information centers.

There's no shortage of bars and pubs in Geneva, and they range from the trendy rooftop hangouts and über-cool cocktail lounges of the five-star lakeside hotels to mellow wine bars and laidback locals' pubs.

Le Rouge et Le Blanc wine bar (27 quai des Bergues; www.lerougeblanc.ch; ✆ **022/731 15 50**), as its name suggests, is an ideal place to try out some local wines beside the river, or try fashionable **Arthur's** (7–9 rue du Rhône; www.arthurs.ch; ✆ **022/810 32 60**), at the heart of the shopping district, with its lovely summer terrace overlooking the Rhône and the lake. I also especially like **La Clémence** (20 Place du Bourg-du-Four; www.laclemence.ch; ✆ **022/312 24 98**), a tiny, wood-paneled watering-hole on the Place du Bourg-du-Four: In winter it serves delicious mulled wine; in summer it boasts ones of the largest sidewalk terraces in the Old Town.

Look no further than **L'Atelier Cocktail Lounge** (rue Henri-Blanvalet 11; ✆ **022/735 22 47.**) or its more casual neighbor, **Yvette de Marseille** (rue Henri-Blanvalet 13; www.yvettedemarseille.ch; ✆ **022/735 15 55**) for creative cocktails; or join the beautiful people in such chic hotel-bar venues as **Le Glow** in Hotel Président Wilson (41 quai Wilson; www.hotelpwilson.com; ✆ **022/906 67 45**) and **Floor Two** (Grand Hotel Kempinski Geneva, Quai du Mont-Blanc 19; www.kempinski.com/en/geneva/grand-hotel-geneva; ✆ **022/908 92 24**) for sophisticated, wallet-walloping cocktails overlooking the lake.

For bars with an after-dark party vibe, it's hard to beat the panoramic outdoor terrace of **Rooftop 42** (42 rue du Rhône; www.rooftop42.com; ✆ **022/346 77 00**) overlooking the lake; or up the beat and head to **Café Cuba** (1 Place du Cirque; www.cafecuba.ch; ✆ **022/328 42 60**), near Pleinpalais, a lively tropical club spread over three floors, where the caipirinhas flow freely and a hip crowd sways to sensual Latin rhythms in a Havana-inspired setting.

Geneva's clubbing scene is vibrant and eclectic. The funky **Au Chat Noir** (13 rue Vautier; www.chatnoir.ch; ✆ **022/307 10 40**) is a veritable institution in the villagey district of Carouge, staging some of Geneva's hottest live music—jazz, funk, hip hop, salsa, and blues performed in a cozy basement club, plus a DJ and a pint-size dance floor.

As most of Geneva sleeps, the chic urban party crowd packs into the Java Club in the basement of the plush Grand Hôtel Kempinski (19 quai du Mont-Blanc; www.javaclub.ch; ✆ **022/908 90 98**) to dance 'til dawn to the hottest house music in town; the atmosphere is hedonistic, the decor deep purple, and the drinks expensive. At the other end of the clubbing spectrum, cult address **L'Usine** (Place des Volontaires 4; www.usine.ch; © **022/781 34 90**), in a former factory, continues to champion the city's alternative clubbing scene with its various concert spaces and varied beats from electro to punk, rock, and metal.

Day Trips from Geneva

Geneva and its lake make an excellent base for touring the surrounding region, and a perfect springboard into France. The lake fringes two countries, and three Swiss cantons (Geneva, Vaud, and Valais).

Step east to discover the resorts of the northern shore, in particular the "Swiss Riviera" from Lausanne to Montreux, renowned for its spectacular scenery, Mediterranean-style microclimate and long-standing tradition of tourism.

Explore the "Olympic Capital" of **Lausanne,** Switzerland's third largest city, from the Gothic heights of **Notre-Dame Cathedral** (Place de la Cathédrale; www.cathedrale-lausanne.ch; © **021/316 71 60**) to the elegant waterfront promenade at Ouchy, with its exclusive yachting harbor, beautiful Belle Époque architecture, and **Musée Olympique** (**Olympic Museum;** Quai d'Ouchy 1; www.olympic.org/museum; © **021/621 65 11**).

Try to schedule your visit to the gracious spa town of **Montreux** to coincide with the fabled **Montreux Jazz Festival,** which takes place each July (book tickets in advance at www.montreuxjazz.com). The nearby **Château de Chillon** (Avenue de Chillon 21, Veytaux; www.chillon.ch/en; © **021/966 8910**) counts among Switzerland's most visited sights—a beautiful,

Montreaux Jazz Festival.

medieval castle romantically sited on a rock jutting into the lake, immortalized by countless artists and writers, including Lord Byron in "The Prisoner of Chillon." Excursions to Lausanne, Montreux, and Château de Chillon can be made by road, rail (see p. 55), or boat with the Lake Geneva Navigation Company (www.cgn.ch; ✆ **0848/811 848**), who also operate day-long paddle-steamer cruises around the lake.

Hire a bicycle, put it on the train to Lausanne, and follow the 33km (21-mile) Lavaux Wine Trail from there to Chillon, through the celebrated UNESCO Lavaux vineyard terraces which cling precipitously to the slopes of the lake and afford intoxicating alpine vistas. Or stay more local and vine-hop by car, bike, or tram around Geneva's outlying wine villages: Anières, Céligny, Russin, and Satigny.

The Vineyards of Lavaux

Cross the Franco-Swiss border to the sedate picture book–pretty town of **Annecy** (40 min. by car from Geneva), set beside a crystal-blue lake and against a backdrop of snowcapped mountains, where flower-lined canals lead to its fairytale red-turreted castle, the medieval **Château d'Annecy** (Place du Château; www.patrimoines.agglo-annecy.fr; ✆ **04/50 33 87 30**). Or visit **Chamonix** (1 hr. by car from Geneva). This French ski-resort ranks among the French Alps' top adventure-sports destinations, and boasts some of Europe's finest mountain hiking.

LUCERNE

by Teresa Fisher

4

Lucerne (*Luzern* in German) and its magnificent lake represent the very essence of Switzerland, located at the heart of Switzerland not only geographically and historically, but also spiritually. For this is storybook Switzerland, the fabled homeland of William Tell, where the seeds were sown in 1291 that led to the Swiss Confederation (see box p. 112). Little wonder that this historic city, with its world-class museums, rich cultural scene, and fairytale setting—beside a vast, shimmering lake and against a rugged backdrop of dense green forests and snowcapped mountains—is one of Switzerland's most popular tourist destinations.

Essentials

The **Lucerne Tourist Office** website is www.luzern.com.

ARRIVING   Lucerne has excellent train connections. Situated at the junction of four major rail lines, it is connected with every other major city in Switzerland by fast train. Allow 50 minutes from Zurich, 1½ hours from Bern, and around 3 hours from Geneva. Call ✆ **0900/300 300** (www.sbb.ch) for rail schedules.

If you're driving from the Swiss capital, Bern, take the A1 north then the A2 to Lucerne (allow 1 hr.). From Zurich, head south and west along the A4, which links into the A14 to Lucerne (allow 1 hr.).

CITY LAYOUT   Most visitors arrive at the train station, on **Bahnhofplatz,** on the left (south) bank of the **River**

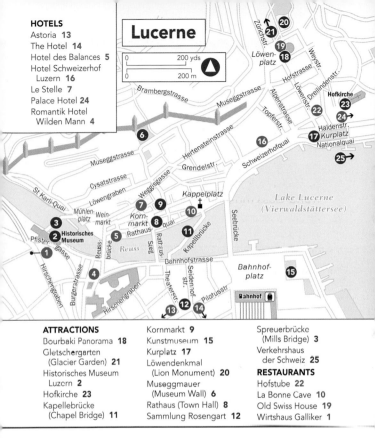

Lucerne

0 200 yds
0 200 m

Zürichstr. **20**
21
19
Löwen- **18**
platz
Weystr.
Hofstrasse Löwengraben Dreilindenstr.

Brambergstrasse
Museggstrasse
Alpenstrasse
Töpferstr.
Hofkirche
22 **23**
Haldenstr.
17 Kurplatz
Nationalquai
25

Museggstrasse
Hertensteinstrasse
6
16
Schweizerhofquai
Grendelstr.

Cysatstrasse
Löwengraben
Weggisgasse
Kappelplatz
St Karli-Quai
Mühlen- Wein-
platz markt
Korn-
3 markt
2 Historisches
Museum
Pfister- gasse
1
Hirschengraben
Burgerstrasse
Reuss- brücke
Reuss
Rathaus- Steg
Dahnhofstrasse
Theaterstr.
Seidenhof- str.
Pilatusstr.
Hirschengraben
4
7 **9**
5 **8**quai
10
11
Kapellbrücke
Seebrücke
Bahnhof- platz
Bahnhof 🚂
15
13 **12** **14**

Lake Lucerne
(Vierwaldstättersee)

Reuss. Immediately, you will see the famous covered
wooden bridge across the river, the early 14th-century
Kapellbrücke (**Chapel Bridge;** see p. 106)—the
city symbol which adorns so many of the local guidebooks, postcards, and chocolate boxes. Farther down-
stream, a second wooden bridge—the **Spreuerbrücke**
(**Mill Bridge),** with gable paintings depicting scenes

99

Kornmarket

from The Dance of Death, was built in 1407 and restored in the 19th century.

Across the river lies the town center and the **Altstadt (Old Town),** the medieval heart of Lucerne, which contains many of the city's most appealing buildings, shops, cafes, and restaurants. Its maze of pedestrianized, cobbled streets and ancient squares is best explored on foot. Look out for the arcaded **Rathaus (Old Town Hall),** dating from 1602, with its typically Swiss roof and Italian Renaissance–style facade—in **Kornmarkt (Corn Market),** site of the weekly market (on Tues and Sat mornings).

Kurplatz marks the main departure point for steamboats tours to visit the various lakeside resorts. The Gothic-Renaissance **Hofkirche (Court Church)** here, with its distinctive twin towers on the site of an earlier monastery, is Lucerne's largest and most important church. Its finely carved doors feature the city's two patron saints, St. Leodegar and St. Maurice, and its arcades house the remains of many of the city's important families. An attractive tree-lined promenade leads from here to the **Verkehrshaus der Schweiz (Swiss Transport Museum;** see p. 110), and the city **Lido**—with its restaurant, play area, beach volleyball, and swimming pool—often dubbed Lucerne's "Riviera," is a favorite summer destination for families.

North of the lake, marvel at the **Bourbaki Panorama** (Löwenplatz 11; www.bourbakipanorama.ch; 9am–6pm), one of the largest canvases in Europe, covering a remarkable curved area of 1,009 sq. m. (10,861 sq. ft.), and painted by Genevois artist Edouard Castres. Not for the faint-hearted, it depicts in great detail the bloody retreat of the French army into Switzerland during the Franco-Prussian war of 1870 to 1871—an event still hailed as one of the finest acts of humanitarian courage in Swiss history.

Just around the corner in Denkmalstrasse is the **Löwendenkmal (Lion Monument),** Lucerne's second most visited site (after the Kapellbrücke). This fatally wounded lion, carved into sandstone rocks, is

A view of Lucerne from the Kapellbrücke (Chapel Bridge).

dedicated to the numerous Swiss mercenaries who died in the French Revolution of 1789. Mark Twain described the dying lion as "the saddest and most moving piece of rock in the world." Children are always fascinated by the **Gletschergarten (Glacier Garden;** Denkmalstrasse 4; Apr–Oct 9am–6pm, Nov–Mar 10am–5pm), with its 32 extraordinary potholes (measuring up to 9m/30 ft. deep and wide) that were worn into the sandstone bed of an Iron Age glacier during the era when ice covered the surface of Lake Lucerne.

For some of the best city vistas, walk the medieval ramparts (**Museggmauer, Museum Wall**) past the city's nine lookout towers. The most scenic stretch is from Wachtturm to the Zytturm, which contains the city's oldest clock. Bizarrely, since medieval times, it has chimed 1 minute ahead of all the other public clocks in Lucerne.

GETTING AROUND   You'll soon feel at home in this charming, laidback city—it's an idyllic town for strolling and lingering, especially on the lakeshore and in the cobbled maze of streets which make up the picturesque Altstadt (Old Town). It's surprisingly compact to explore on foot. However, it's equally easy to explore by **bus** (one ride costs between CHF2–CHF6, depending on the distance you ride). There are route maps and automatic vending machines at the bus stops. A 24-hour ticket costs CHF30.

For outlying attractions, it's hard to resist traveling by **boat** (see p. 104). Lake Lucerne's fleet of beautifully restored steamboats provide links between many small lakeside communities and attractions, some of which are still more easily reached by boat than by any other mode of transport.

The Hofkirche, Lucerne.

Bikes can be rented at the railway station for CHF27/CHF35 per half-day/full-day or CHF39/CHF54 per half-day/full-day for an E-bike. See www.rentabike.ch for details and online reservations. The shores of the lake are perfect for bike rides—get a map from the tourist office, and take a picnic! The trail along the southern shore is especially scenic. Set off from the train station toward Tribschen, venue of the **Richard Wagner Museum** ★ (see p. 113), St-Niklausen and Kastanienbaum. If you have time, continue on to Winkel-Horw beach for a dip in the lake. Allow a couple of hours for the 18km (11 mile) roundtrip.

Exploring Lucerne

Thanks to its unique mix of history, culture, folklore, lakes, and mountains, the city of Lucerne is Switzerland at its scenic best. This medieval gem was one of the first Swiss cities to be discovered by 19th-century philosophers, painters, and poets who, wooed by its charm and grandiose scenery, put it on the map of Europe as a stylish resort. Still today, it remains hugely popular, a picturesque city with all the charm and intimacy of a small town, just a stone's throw from Zurich and Bern, at the gateway to the high Alps.

LUCERNE'S lake

Lucerne's vast, glacial lake is the fourth-largest in Switzerland. It is 38km (24-miles) long and at its broadest 3.3km (2-miles) wide, with numerous fjords and finger-like inlets, flanked by dramatic limestone outcrops, steep forested gorges, and towering mountains. It's known in German as the *Vierwaldstättersee* and in French as the *Lac des Quatre Cantons*, the "lake of the four forest states" (Lucerne, Uri, Unterwalden, and Schwyz), and many consider it Europe's most beautiful and romantic lake. It's hugely popular for walking and watersports, including waterskiing, sailing, and swimming in its popular lidos, and also for its many paddle steamers, which ply between the many small lakeside communities, some of which are more easily reached by boat than by any other means of transport.

Lucerne is the ideal base for nostalgic paddle-steamer excursions into the surrounding "William Tell Country." Some of the resorts hugging the lakeside get very crowded in high season, especially those closest to Lucerne, so I suggest you skip the tourist honeypots of Weggis and Vitznau and head farther afield to explore the narrow inlet of **Urnersee** at the southeastern tip of Lake Lucerne, which not only attracts fewer visitors than

Alongside its top-class museums and cultural venues, take time to explore the Altstadt (Old Town), with its narrow cobbled streets, covered bridges, frescoed houses, historical buildings, and fountains; to stroll beside the clear blue waters of Lake Lucerne; and to walk the medieval ramparts for spectacular views across the rooftops of the town to the majestic, snowcapped mountains beyond.

Historisches Museum Luzern ★ MUSEUM Kids especially love the eclectic displays of artifacts in this quirky History Museum—lovingly dubbed "The Depot"

other parts of the lake, but also boasts some of its wildest and most majestic scenery. Here also you'll find a giant natural rock obelisk, the **Schillerstein**—dedicated to Friedrich von Schiller, author of *Wilhelm Tell*—which rises some 25 m (82 ft.) out of the lake.

Schiffahrtsgesellschaft Vierwaldstättersee (Lake Lucerne Navigation Co.; www.lakelucerne.ch; ✆ **041/ 367 67 67**) operates Europe's largest flotilla of lake steamers in and out of Lucerne. A return passage to the lake's most distant point, Flüelen (allow 4 hr.), costs CHF72 and departs from the quays opposite the Hauptbahnhof in Lucerne. Tickets for shorter hops are calculated according to their distance (CHF38 to Weggis and back, CHF45 for Vitznau). In midsummer, departures begin at 9:15am and continue every hour or so throughout the day.

Wherever you choose to disembark, be sure to find out the departure time of the last boat back to Lucerne. The last boat from Flüelen usually departs before 4pm. All boats have a restaurant, or at least a cafeteria, onboard. Scheduled cruises are free if you have a Swiss Card or Eurail train pass, and half-price for InterRail pass holders.

by locals and housed in a former 16th-century arsenal— largely because they get the chance to wave a bar-code- reading hand-held scanner over key items in order to find out information about each object (in English). It is an excellent first port of call, covering every aspect of city life from history and local folklore and fashion to toys and religious relics. Once you have a grasp of Lucerne's colorful history, walks around town are all the more rewarding. Pfistergasse 24. www.historischesmuseum.lu.ch. ✆ **041/228 54 24.** CHF10 adults, CHF8 seniors, CHF5 children aged 6 to 16, free for children under 6. Bus: 2 or 12. Tues–Sun 10am–5pm.

Mount Pilatus

Few visitors to the Lucerne area return home without first climbing one of the nearby mountains to see the lake at its finest. Rigi is popular, with dazzling vistas over the lake and Lucerne (accessed via the Rigi Railway from Weggis or Vitznau, www.rigi.ch), but it's hard to beat Pilatus (www.pilatus.ch), 15km (9 miles) south of Lucerne, for the best 360-degree views of central Switzerland. Simply hop aboard a boat to Alpnachstadt (the journey takes around 90 min.) and then the steepest electric **cogwheel railway** in the world—running at a 48% gradient—will whisk you to the top of Mount Pilatus (2,132m/6,994 ft.) in just 30 minutes, where a large sun terrace and two restaurants serve up breathtaking vistas with their traditional Swiss fare. Be forewarned however: The summit is often cloud-covered (hence its name, which is thought to originate from the Latin *pileatus*, meaning "capped"), so try to visit as early as possible in the day for the best chance of a decent view. Many choose to make a circular trip and descent by cable car. If you have family, it's worth pausing at **Fräkmüntegg,** where the **Seilpark Pilatus**—a suspension rope park with aerial cablewalks, log bridges, and ziplines—provides hours of fun, followed by a ride on the **Fräkgaudi Rodelbahn,** a 1,350m (4,429 ft.) toboggan run, the longest summer run in Switzerland. From Fräkmüntegg, another cable car descends to Kriens for a short connecting bus ride back to Lucerne.

Kapellbrücke (Chapel Bridge) ★★★ BRIDGE
The Chapel Bridge is Europe's oldest covered wooden footbridge and the most photographed building in Switzerland. The major events which shaped the country over the centuries are portrayed in a series of flamboyant Renaissance wall paintings under the roof of the bridge, together with scenes from the lives of the city's two patron saints, St. Leodegar and St. Maurice.

Imagine how upset the locals were when much of their beloved bridge burned down in 1993. It has since been lovingly restored, many of the wall paintings have been reproduced, and the bridge continues to welcome tourists galore. Dominating the bridge, the even older **Wasserturm (Water Tower,** closed to the public) dates from around 1300. Over the years, this octagonal structure has been variously used as an archive, treasury, prison, and torture chamber.

Kapellbrücke. Free. Hauptbahnhof. Open 24 hours.

Kunstmuseum ★ MUSEUM   The Museum of Art is housed in the impressive metal-and-glass KKL Luzern (Lucerne Culture & Convention Center) which dominates the waterfront with its huge overhanging roof, designed by the French architect Jean Nouvel. There is no permanent collection on view here, but rather a rolling program of temporary exhibitions. Depending on the themes, you may get to see some of the museum's own contemporary Swiss art and historic landscape collections—including important works by Swiss artist Ferdinand Hodler.

Europaplatz 1. www.kunstmuseumluzern.ch. ℂ **041/226 78 00.** CHF15 adults, CHF6 children 6–16, free children under 6. Bus: any to the main train station. Tues–Sun 10am–6pm (Wed to 8pm).

The wooden Kapellbrücke (Chapel Bridge).

LOCAL passes

Museum buffs will benefit from the 2-day **Luzern Museum Card** (see www.luzern.com for info), which, for CHF36 per person, gives unlimited access to all the main museums for 2 consecutive days. Even if you're only planning on visiting the Swiss Transport Museum and one other, it's worth your while.

Also, if you stay overnight in Lucerne, you will receive a free **Visitors Card** from your accommodation, which gives you discounts on a number of excursions, museums, boat trips, and cable cars in the region.

If you plan to explore the region, travel around the Vierwaldstättersee is made simple by the **Tell Pass,** which provides unlimited travel on public transport (train, bus, and boat) for a minimum of 2 days (from CHF100). It covers most mountain railways, although some have an additional alpine surcharge.

Sammlung Rosengart ★★★ MUSEUM It's a family affair at Samm-lung Rosengart—a stunning collection of 19th- and 20th-century artworks housed in a grand neoclassical former bank building that dates from 1924. Art dealer Siegfried Rosengart, who moved to Lucerne after World War I, was friends with many leading artists including Klee, Chagall, Matisse, and Picasso. Together with his daughter Angela, he amassed and donated to the town an astonishing collection, containing hundreds of works by many of the great modern artists, including Bonnard, Braque, Cézanne, Chagall, Kandinsky, Klee, Matisse, Monet, Pissarro, and Renoir—it is a truly remarkable collection. The whole of the ground floor and several of the first-floor rooms are devoted to Picasso and include 32 paintings and 100 drawings, watercolors and sculptural works, including

THE TALE OF william tell

The Vierwaldstättersee region is the fabled homeland of Switzerland's national hero, William Tell. Over the centuries, the character of William Tell has become one of the most famous names in Swiss history—symbolizing the struggle for political and individual freedom, and inextricably linked with the founding of the Swiss Confederation, although there is no proof for his actual existence. According to legend, Tell was a simple man from the village of Bürglen, near Urnersee (Lake Uri), one of the inlets of the Vierwaldstättersee. He was arrested by a tyrannical Habsburg bailiff named Gessler, who threatened to execute him unless he could prove his skill as a marksman by shooting an arrow through an apple on his own son's head.

The story goes that Tell successfully split the apple in two but then confessed to having a second arrow, meant for Gessler had his son been injured. Furious, the bailiff refused to free him but took him on a boat ride instead, headed for jail in Küssnacht. During the voyage, a sudden storm blew up and Tell, with his local knowledge of the Vierwaldstättersee, was released to steer the boat to safety. He escaped by jumping ashore near Sisikon, and pushed the boat and its crew back out into the middle of the stormy lake. He later ambushed Gessler, when he finally came ashore, shooting him through the heart with his last arrow. The Tollskapelle (Tell Chapel) stands today on the shore of the Urnersee (Lake Uri), between Sisikon and Flüelen, as a monument to the beloved Swiss hero.

five portraits of Angela who, now in her 80s, still runs the museum. Another highlight is the extensive collection of photographs of Picasso at work and play, taken by American photographer David Douglas Duncan. Pilatusstrasse 10. www.rosengart.ch. ✆ **041/22016 60.** CHF18 adult, CHF10 children 7–16, free children under 6. Bus: 1. Nov–Mar daily 11am–5pm, Apr–Oct daily 10am–6pm.

Verkehrshaus der Schweiz (Swiss Transport Museum) ★★★ MUSEUM Switzerland's most popular museum and the largest of its kind on the continent, the Swiss Transport Museum is really not as geeky as it sounds. It covers every imaginable form of transport from old rolling stock, vintage aircraft and racing cars, ski lifts and spaceships, plus a wonderfully eccentric Road Transport Hall, decorated by 344 road signs. The sections on trains, shipping, and tunnel building are almost entirely Swiss-oriented, but those on air, road, and space travel have a more international flavor. The museum has been considerably expanded since it opened in 1959, with the addition of entire new buildings and an IMAX cinema, and there are lots of hands-on and multimedia exhibits which are fun for young and old: Climb inside an old airliner, or tour Switzerland in just a few steps via the walk-on aerial map, with a gigantic mobile magnifying glass to spot key sights. From train driving to space-travel simulation in the planetarium, it's hardly surprising the museum draws over a million visitors annually. However, it never really feels busy—the site is so huge, it even offers bicycles to its public. If you plan to make a day of it, there's a simple cafe as well as a more formal restaurant. It is situated a short bus or boat ride away from the main train station or a 30-minute walk along the quayside from the Old Town. Lidostrasse 5. www.verkehrshaus.ch. ℂ **041/370 44 44.** CHF30 adults, CHF15 children 6–16, children under 6 free; with IMAX film CHF40 adults, CHF25 children. Bus: 6, 8, or 24 to Verkehrshaus stop; train: S3 or Voralpenexpress to Luzern Verkehrshaus stop; boat: to Verkehrshaus Lido. Apr–Oct daily 10am–6pm, Nov–Mar daily 10am–5pm.

HEADING OUTDOORS

The surrounding countryside yields endless hiking opportunities, and the most famous hike in the region,

Formula One racing cars in the Swiss Transport Museum.

with exceptional panoramas of the majestic mountains around the Vierwaldstättersee and beyond, is the **Weg der Schweiz (Swiss Path)** ★★★—an easy 36km (22 miles) walk that loops around the Urnersee (Lake Uri)—which was designed in 1991 to celebrate the 700th anniversary of the Swiss Confederation, which took place in the meadows nearby (see p. 112). Each of the 26 sections of the walk represents a different canton, in the order they joined the Confederation; the length of each stretch is directly proportionate to the number of residents in that canton—every 5mm (⅕ of an inch) represents a Swiss citizen. The trail starts, aptly enough, at Switzerland's birthplace, the Rütli Meadow, although you can join it at any point. The entire path is easily manageable in 2 days, and English-language guide maps of the route are available from local tourist offices.

Where to Stay

As one of Switzerland's most visited cities, Lucerne offers a wide range of hotels. But they're mostly expensive or, at best, moderately priced; there's a distinct shortage of good budget hotels. Advance reservations are especially important during summer months.

111

Birth of the Swiss Nation

Following the death of the mighty Habsburg ruler, King of Germany and Holy Roman Emperor Rudolph I in 1291, who had heavy-handedly governed much of northern Switzerland, the Swiss people faced an uncertain future, so they decided it was time to secure their own destiny. This led to a series of revolts, which resulted in the forging of new allegiances. The most important partnership made that year was the League of the Three Forest Cantons. It is believed that representatives of three of the nation's most powerful cantons—Uri, Unterwalden, and Schwyz (from which Switzerland derives its name)—met at the Rütli Meadow on the west shore of the Urnersee. Together they secured a historic victory in 1315, defeating the Habsburgs at the Battle of Morgarten. They officially recorded their union of three cantons as the **"Swiss Confederation"**; their land collectively became known as Schwyz and its people became Schwyzers. Support grew over the next 2 centuries, as gradually each canton joined the Swiss Confederation, known in Latin as the *Confoederatio Helvetica*. To this day, the abbreviation CH is used to denote Switzerland.

EXPENSIVE

The Hotel ★★★   Jean Nouvel, French "starchitect" and designer of the city's landmark KKL (see p. 107) has cleverly converted this old townhouse into an ultra-modern boutique hotel, with minimalist decor and splashy cinematic displays. Every inch of space has been lovingly thought through: Big windows take advantage of the natural light and the hotel's position near a leafy park, while minimalist bathrooms make the most of their dimensions, and each of the 30 rooms has custom-designed furnishings. Choose from four types of accommodation: deluxe studios, corner junior suites, garden and park loft suites (with patios), and penthouse junior suites (roof terrace, great views of the city and mountains). The onsite restaurant **Bam Bou ★,** with its innovative pan-Asian menu and slick decor, makes a pleasant change from Swiss cuisine.

Sempacherstrasse 14. www.the-hotel.ch. ✆ **041/226 86 86.** Doubles CHF370, suites CHF430–CHF750. Bus: 7, 8, 14, or 20. **Amenities:** Restaurant; bar; babysitting; room service; free Wi-Fi.

Hotel Schweizerhof Luzern ★★★ The iconic neo-Renaissance-style Schweizerhof stands sentinel over Lucerne's eponymously named Schweizer-hofquai, secure in the knowledge that it remains one of the city's best loved landmarks. Run by the same family for five generations, there's a homespun charm to the service here, despite all the luxury trappings

---

Richard Wagner

The German composer came to live near Lucerne in Hauz Tribschen on the southern shore of the lake in 1866, together with Cosima von Bülow, the daughter of Franz Liszt, whom he married 4 years later. His elegant lakeside villa, with its green shutters and verdant sloping lawns, has been converted into the **Richard Wagner Museum ★** (Wagnerweg 27, Tribschen, CH-6005; www.richard-wagner-museum.ch; ✆ **041/360 23 70**), complete with historic musical instruments, original scores, letters, photos, and various memorabilia belonging to the great maestro. Here, beside the lake, Wagner composed some of his finest opera music, including *Die Meistersinger von Nürnberg* and parts of his epic *Ring Cycle.* Located a short walk from the city center along a scenic lakeside path (allow 30 min. each way), a visit here is a must for all opera buffs.

The Hotel Schweizerhof.

such as the beautifully preserved marble-columned lobby and the snazzy bar; and the rooms artfully combine character with all mod cons. Opera buffs, take note that Richard Wagner wrote *Tristan and Isolde* here in 1859.

Schweizerhofquai 3. www.schweizerhof-luzern.ch. ✆ **041/410 04 10.** 101 units. Doubles CHF360–CHF600, suites CHF600–CHF880. Bus: 1, 6, 8 or 24. **Amenities:** 2 restaurants; bar; baby-sitting; gym; sauna; room service; free Wi-Fi.

Palace Hotel ★★★ The undisputed jewel in the crown, the five-star Palace Hotel is indeed a Belle Epoque beauty—a regal blend of period details and modern refinements, seamlessly held together by sterling service. Think high ceilings, marble columns, warm-hued luxury fabrics, original marble floors, a chic terrace, and dreamy views over the lake. Each room is individually decorated: Some are highly traditional, others boldly modern, and some a mix of the two. There's also a sensational spa, and one of the top restaurants in town, **Jasper ★★★**—where all ingredients are sourced in Switzerland and every plate of perfectly prepared modern Mediterranean cuisine is a culinary marvel, matched by an exemplary wine list.

Haldenstrasse 10. www.palace-luzern.ch. © **041/416 16 16.** 129 units. Low season Doubles CHF352–CHF602, suites CHF552–CHF1,560. Bus: 6, 8, or 24. **Amenities:** 2 restaurants; bar; concierge; spa and fitness; room service; free Wi-Fi.

MODERATE

Astoria ★   From its reception area's icy design ethos to its superior conference facilities, the Astoria targets business travelers. However, its 90 deluxe "Design" rooms, with their minimalist cache and trendy white-on-white decor, are a cut above your average business hotel. Designed by Switzerland's famous Herzog & de Meuron firm, each room features timber flooring, rain showers, and other designer touches. Located close to the Old Town center and a very short stroll to the Sammlung Rosengart, the KKL, and main train station, the Astoria is also ideal for those not looking to travel too far when it comes to dining well. Of several restaurants, our favorite is **La Cucina ★★,** which oozes Italian theatricality and atmosphere, with its exuberant waiters who know that performance is part of the charm; and a delicious menu of homemade pasta and pizzas cooked in a wood-fired oven. At lunchtime, it's very popular with people doing business, and offers a better than average set-price lunch menu. Reservations advised.

Pilatusstrasse 29. www.astoria-luzern.ch. © **041/226 88 88.** 252 units. Doubles from CHF270. Bus: 1. **Amenities:** 5 restaurants; 2 bars; babysitting; gym; room service; free Wi-Fi.

Hotel des Balances ★★   This four-star hotel has one of the Altstadt's best locations; its front entrance opens onto a picturesque fountain-splashed square, its buildings adorned with vibrant frescoes, while its back

Exterior of the Hotel des Balances.

entrance faces the Reuss River, with stunning views over to the Chapel Bridge and Jesuit Church. Inside, the sleek rooms (which face onto either the river or the square) blend modern comforts with high-end contemporary design, gilt-framed mirrors, parquet flooring, and lots of white and neutral tones. Suites are decorated in a similar style, and some have wrought-iron balconies. **Des Balances restaurant ★★** is a firm favorite with locals and a highlight of any stay, especially the five- or seven-course set menu of seasonal European cuisine. Book in advance for a table on the riverside terrace.

Weinmarkt 4. www.balances.ch. ✆ **041/418 28 28.** 56 units. Doubles CHF350–CHF430, suites CHF430–CHF630. Bus: 1, 6, or 8. **Amenities:** Restaurant; bar; baby-sitting; room service; free Wi-Fi.

Romantik Hotel Wilden Mann ★★ The oldest building in this intimate complex of seven townhouses dates from 1517, so the much-loved Wilden Mann ("Wild Man"), a warrenlike and character-filled hotel brimming with nostalgic charm, is a must for those looking to revel in Lucerne's old-fashioned charm. The

50 cozy, individually decorated rooms and suites feature original antiques, wooden beams, four-poster beds, warm colors, and embossed fabrics. Its location in the city's Old Town, within walking distance of the city's major sights and historic delights makes it a great choice, and its two very good restaurants only seal the deal. The **Burgerstube ★★** is especially atmospheric, with its wood-paneled dining room, coffered ceiling, coats of arms, and hunting trophies. The menu veers away from the usual formula by presenting regional and traditional ingredients with an imaginative twist; the fixed-price menus are an excellent value for money. Bahnhofstrasse 30. www.wilden-mann.ch. ℭ **041/210 16 66.** 50 units. Doubles CHF310–CHF425, suites CHF360–CHF490. Bus: 1. **Amenities:** 2 restaurants; baby-sitting; room service; free Wi-Fi.

INEXPENSIVE

Le Stelle ★   Le Stelle brings some much needed boutique hotel oomph to the historic center of town, although it's a tiny place whose rooms (singles and doubles only) don't leave much space for anything other than guests and their luggage (hence no children can stay at the hotel, because there's no room for a cot). Decor is subtle, modern, and minimal, with gleaming white paint and bedding, plus Moroccan tiling details in the bathrooms, and some rooms even feature period details such as wooden beams. The small on-site restaurant serves Italian food and has a little terrace out front, which is perfect for soaking up the ambience of Old Town. Check-in takes place at the nearby Hotel Krone (Weinmarkt 12). Hirschenplatz 3. www.lestelle.ch. ℭ **041/412 22 20.** 10 units. Doubles CHF230–CHF320. Bus: 1. **Amenities:** restaurant; free Wi-Fi.

Where to Eat

Lucerne has some excellent restaurants to suit all budgets, so don't confine yourself to your hotel at mealtimes (although, that said, some of the finest restaurants are situated in the city's hotels, so check out the "Where to Stay" listings, too).

Given the high number of visitors, most restaurants are open all day, and many offer alfresco dining in summer. During your stay, be sure to try the local specialty, the *Lozärner Chügelipastete*—a large puff-pastry filled with veal in a cream and mushroom sauce.

EXPENSIVE

Old Swiss House ★★ EUROPEAN   Don't be put off by the tour groups galore eating at this landmark half-timbered building near the Lion Monument—it's a veritable culinary institution run by the Buholzer family since 1931, and on many people's must-visit list for its impeccable staff attired in traditional costume, serving a feast of Swiss and European fare. The 40,000-strong wine cellar and such irresistible dishes as Zurich-style veal in a cream sauce served with rösti, or Wienerschnitzel prepared and cooked at your table, should be enough to impress most diners, but the interior decorations that date to the 17th century (hand-carved wall panels, solid oak doors, oil paintings, stained-glass windows, and a porcelain-tiled stove) do their best to distract. Reservations are essential.

Löwenplatz 4. www.oldswisshouse.ch. © **041/410 61 71.** Mains CHF28–CHF69. Bus: 1, 18, 19, 22, or 23. Tues–Sun 9am–12:30am.

MODERATE

Hofstube ★ SWISS/FRENCH   Join locals and visitors at the popular half-timbered Hotel Zum Rebstock in the Old Town to tuck into an array of food

Lamb and chicken with truffled leeks at the Old Swiss House.

specialties from central Switzerland and France. There are several characterful dining areas to choose from, depending on your mood: the elegant older dining room, or Hofstube, boasts period details and white napery; the newer, more intimate Hofegge is ideal for a quiet tête-à-tête; while the Wirtshuus dining area has a low-key, more casual feel. Wherever you sit, the menu's the same, with a particularly good selection of warming soups and copious salads. In summer, there's a lively terrace and verdant garden for alfresco dining, and on Sundays a popular brunch (CHF30) is served from 7am to 2:30pm. Reservations recommended.

Sankt-Leodegar-Platz 3. www.rebstock-luzern.ch. ✆ **041/417 18 19.** Mains CHF23–CHF58. Bus: 1, 6, 7, or 8. Daily 11:30am–11:30pm, Sun brunch 7:30am–2:30pm.

Wirtshaus Galliker ★★ SWISS Run by the same family for four generations, this is one of Lucerne's best-loved spots for generous portions of unfussy but delicious local cuisine, heartily served in a traditionally decorated atmosphere that encourages the feeling you've left the modern world and all its travails behind. With all that wood paneling, grandmotherly service, floral curtains, and a talkative local crowd, you'd be mad not to try the Lucerne veal specialty dish, *Chügelipastete,* or something even more substantial, such as calf's head, or local sausages seasoned with caraway seeds. Reservations are advised.

Schützenstrasse 1. ✆ **041/240 10 02.** Mains CHF25–CHF55. Bus: 2, 9, or 12. Tues–Sat 9:30am–midnight.

INEXPENSIVE

La Bonne Cave ★ SWISS/ITALIAN Medieval stone vaulting, a stone floor and, as the name suggests, wine wherever your gaze falls sets the scene here, with dozens of vintages from Switzerland and around the world to heighten your mood. Alongside its fine wines, The Good Cellar serves up some good-value midday meals, satisfying pasta dishes, and nice platters of antipasti and Swiss charcuterie (with Bresaola, salami, dried ham, chorizo, olive oil, and pickled vegetables). Menus come with wine suggestions, and bottles from the attached wine shop can be bought to open with your meal. It's a lovely Old Town spot near Reuss River and the Chapel Bridge, with a dash of boho charm and romance come evening, when the candles are lit and the lights are turned low.

Rathausquai 1. www.weinwirtschaft.ch. ✆ **041/410 45 16.** Mains CHF18–CHF38. Bus: 1, 6, or 8. Mon, Wed–Fri 11:30am–10pm; Tues 10am–10pm; Sat 8am–10pm; Sun 8am–8pm.

Shopping

Shopping in Lucerne relies heavily upon the tourist trade, so expect a mass of touristy boutiques on virtually every street corner. Look closer, however, and you will spot some classic shops selling high-quality goods. For Swiss timepieces, you won't beat **Bucherer,** Schwanenplatz 5 (www.bucherer.com; ✆ **041/369 77 00**), the biggest jeweler in town, for choice and quality, but also a large price tag.

Schweizer Heimatwerk, at Kapellgasse 3 (www.heimatwerk.ch; ✆ **041/266 07 36**), admirably demonstrates that the country has considerably more to offer than cows and edelweiss, with its fine selection of beautiful handicrafts made by Swiss artists and artisans, including pottery, kitchenware, clothing, glassware, and toys. For a quirkier souvenir, **Hofstetter & Berney,** Schweizerhofquai 6 (© **041/410 31 06**), have a splendid collection of music boxes. The staff will tell you about the differences in tones and the complexities of sounds produced by the various instruments, all of which are made in Switzerland and which contain varying numbers of musical notes. Also, on the first Saturday of the month, there's a craft fair at the **Weinmarkt,** where you can pick up some unique, locally made gifts.

Foodies will enjoy picnic-shopping at the outdoor fruit and vegetable market on the banks of the river every Tuesday and Saturday (except in winter) from 8am to 1pm; and don't miss a visit to **Confiserie H & M Kurmann,** Bahnhofstrasse 7 (www.art-confiserie-kurmann.ch; © **041/210 19 18**), the most distinguished pastry-and-chocolate shop in Lucerne, with its mouthwatering displays of highly calorific and highly tempting cakes and pastries. Look out also for their masterly chocolate edifices: Just think . . . the city's Watertower, the Old Town Hall, or the Lion Monument made out of chocolate would make a lovely present to take home, if it wasn't just too tempting to eat straight away!

Entertainment & Nightlife

There's something for everyone after dark in Lucerne. Beer lovers should head straight to **Rathaus Bräuerei** (Unter der Egg 2; www.braui-luzern.ch) near the Chapel Bridge on the riverfront—a tavern that brews its own refreshingly light Pilsner and a rich and malty Bockbier on-site. Our favorite—a blond lager called Rathaus Bier—goes down surprisingly well accompanied by a giant pretzel or one of their hearty platefuls of local sausages and schnitzels.

For an evening of alphorns, cowbells, national costumes, flag-throwing, yodeling, and more, traditionalists will enjoy the folkloric Swiss entertainment at the jolly but undeniably touristy **Stadtkeller** (Sternenplatz 3; www.swissfolkloreshow.com). Both are located in the **Altstadt** (Old Town), together with a clutch of cozy bars and cafes.

You'll find some of the more sophisticated night spots in the hotels: sip cocktails at ultra-cool **Blue** (in the Renaissance Lucerne Hotel, Pilatussstrasse 15) or rub shoulders with Lucerne's beautiful people at **Lounge Bar** (in The Hotel; see p. 112). The **Louis Bar** (in the Art Deco Hotel Montana, Adligenswilerstrasse 22; www.hotel-montana.ch; ✆ **041/419 00 00**), named after the legendary jazz trumpeter Louis Armstrong, boasts over 90 single malt whiskeys and occasional impromptu music sessions.

Party animals will enjoy the hip **Loft** nightclub (Haldenstrasse 2; www.theloft.ch; ✆ **041/410 92 44**); the trendy late-night party vibe and sensational

Kultur und Kongress Zentrum.

bird's-eye city views at the **Suite Lounge** (at the top of Hotel Monopol—expect to queue at weekends, Pilatusstrasse 1; www.monopolluzern.ch; ☏ **041/226 43 43**) with its open-air terraces; or the more sophisticated atmosphere (and equally splendid aerial views) of the **Penthouse Rooftop Bar** (in the Astoria hotel; see p. 115), which is perfect for early evening sundowners, or for late nights on weekends when DJs get everyone in the party mood.

For something altogether more highbrow, head for the **KKL** (**Kultur und Kongress Zentrum Luzern/Culture & Convention Center;** Europaplatz 1; www.kkl-luzern.ch; ☏ **041/226 77 77** [box office]; see p. 107). Lucerne's eye-catching postmodern performing arts center on the lake was designed by Parisian architect Jean Nouvel and boasts state-of-the-art acoustics that rank among the best in the world. Its angular glass-and-metal edifice, with a gigantic copper-sheathed roof, sits in stark contrast to the spires and cute alpine architecture of the rest of town; and its year-round entertainment program, spanning from rock and pop to classical music, includes performances from the local resident orchestra, the **Allgemeine Musikgesellschaft,** from October to June. Also by the lake on the railway station side of town, the nearby **Stadttheater** (Theaterstrasse 2; www. luzernertheater.ch; ☏ **041/228 14 14**) stages theater in German and operas in their original language.

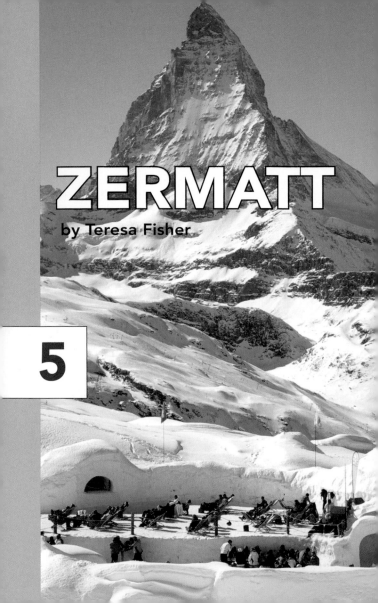

ZERMATT

by Teresa Fisher

5

The picture-postcard mountain village of Zermatt, 1,594m (5,228 ft.) above sea level, is hidden at the top of Switzerland's steepest valley, at the base of the nation's most celebrated mountain—the Matterhorn.

Once a humble farming community, it was put on the map by English mountaineers in the mid-19th century and is now a glamorous resort, especially popular in winter for skiing and snow-sports, but also in summer for mountain hiking—thanks to an impressive ensemble of cable cars, lifts, and cog railways that operates 365 days a year. Zermatt boasts the highest ski area in Europe, with skiing throughout the year on the Theodul glacier at an elevation of up to 3,883m (12,740 ft.).

The village itself is a charming jumble of ancient wooden chalets and huts interspersed with glitzy hotels, restaurants, and shops worthy of a capital city. Hardly surprisingly, it attracts more than its fair share of visitors. You can walk from one end of the village to the other in about 15 minutes, which is handy because it is a car-free village

Essentials

The **Zermatt Tourist Office** website is www.zermatt.ch.

ARRIVING Take a **train** to Visp or Brig, where you can transfer to a narrow-gauge train to Zermatt.

Departures are every 20 minutes daily between 6am and 11:30pm. It takes just over 3 hours from Zurich, and around 4 hours from Geneva. For Swiss **rail information,** call ✆ **0900/300-300** or visit www.sbb.ch.

If you're **driving,** head to Täsch, 4.8km (3 miles) from Zermatt. Because Zermatt is a car-free resort, you need to park your car in the large multi-story carpark at Täsch, and jump on the cog rail shuttle (which stops right beside the carpark) up to the resort. Tickets cost CHF16 per person round-trip (half-price for children aged 6–16).

In addition, **buses** run from Visp and Brig to Täsch hourly to connect with the cog train. See the tourist office website (www.zermatt.ch) for more information.

GETTING AROUND The best way to discover Zermatt is **on foot,** but take care when crossing the road—although the resort is car-free, there are loads of **electric carts** whizzing around. The village is traversed by the River Vispa, with most of the shops and attractions in the vicinity of the main street

Zermatt Valley and the Matterhorn.

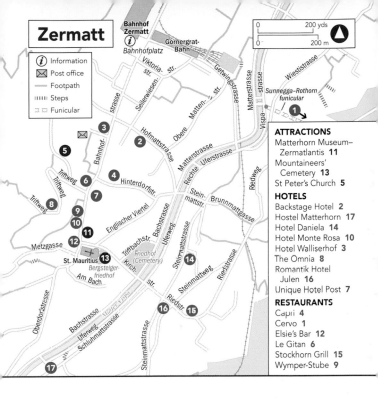

Zermatt

- ⓘ Information
- ✉ Post office
- — Footpath
- ⋯⋯ Steps
- ⊐⊏ Funicular

Bahnhof Zermatt ⓘ
Bahnhofplatz
Gornergrat-Bahn

ATTRACTIONS
Matterhorn Museum–
Zermatlantis **11**
Mountaineers'
Cemetery **13**
St Peter's Church **5**

HOTELS
Backstage Hotel **2**
Hostel Matterhorn **17**
Hotel Daniela **14**
Hotel Monte Rosa **10**
Hotel Walliserhof **3**
The Omnia **8**
Romantik Hotel
Julen **16**
Unique Hotel Post **7**

RESTAURANTS
Capri **4**
Cervo **1**
Elsie's Bar **12**
Le Gitan **6**
Stockhorn Grill **15**
Wymper-Stube **9**

(Bahnhofstrasse), and hotels are well sign-posted. The tourist office at Bahnhofplatz 5 can supply you with maps of the resort as well as hiking/skiing routes in the surrounding mountains.

Many sports shops, such as **Bayard Zermatt** (Bahnhofplatz 2; ℂ **027/966-49-50**), rent **bicycles** as well as skiing, hiking, and climbing equipment and clothing, sledges, and even prams. You can even tour the village year-round by **horse and carriage** with local resident **Werner Imboden** (📞 **079/436-76-12** for a quote).

The comprehensive network of cable cars and the celebrated **Gornergrat** mountain railway (see p. 132) provide easy access to the many ski slopes and hiking trails in the surrounding mountains (see **Mountain Excursions,** p. 132).

Exploring Zermatt

Nestled at the foot of Switzerland's landmark mountain—the majestic 4,478m (14,691-ft.) high Matterhorn—and encircled by majestic snowcapped peaks, Zermatt counts among the world's most famous mountain resorts, famed for its skiing, hiking, and mountaineering; its beautiful boutiques; and some of the Alps' most glamorous hotels.

Aside from the mountains, Zermatt village offers many diversions for its visitors, including a variety of specialist shops and an eclectic mix of bars and restaurants. Its sixteen rinks for ice-skating and curling, and its sledging and ski schools in winter, together with a Forest Fun Park (www.zermatt-fun.ch) of ropeways, high wire walkways, and bridges suspended in the trees (open Easter–Oct), are especially appealing to children.

Matterhorn   Museum-Zermatlantis   ★★★

MUSEUM   Hidden beneath the pavement, within an ugly former casino building, this small but ingenious museum winds the clocks back to times when there were no mountain railways or ski lifts in Zermatt. It documents the rise of this tiny farming community to become one of the world's most glamorous resorts. The museum is cleverly presented as an

Climbing the Matterhorn

World attention first turned to the **Matterhorn** during the 1860s, when English explorer and mountaineer Edward Whymper made a series of attempts to reach the summit. Approaching the Matterhorn from the Italian side, he tried six times and failed. Then, on July 14 1865, after changing his strategy and approaching the mountain from the Swiss side (using Zermatt as his departure point), he succeeded in becoming the first person to reach the elusive summit. It was a fateful expedition however—four climbers in his team fell to their deaths on the descent. Ever since, Zermatt has been a mecca for mountaineers, although only a few attempt to climb the Matterhorn.

archaeological dig, with entire mountain huts reconstructed to show how people lived and worked here in the 19th century. An appealing selection of hands-on exhibits, multimedia, and ancient film footage reveals the story of Switzerland's most photogenic mountain from its dramatic first ascent by Edward Whymper in 1865 (see box above) to the various routes up the Matterhorn for the 3,000-plus alpinists who annually

The scenic Glacier Express railway.

climb this iconic mountain. Allow 1 to 1½ hours to visit.

Kirchplatz 11. www.matterhornmuseum.ch. © **027/967 41 00.** Adults CHF10, children 10–16 CHF5, free for children 9 and under. Train (Zermatt). Open Jan–May daily 3–7pm (Fri until 8pm); June daily 2–6pm; July–Sept daily 11am–6pm; Oct daily 3–6pm; mid-Nov to mid-Dec Fri–Sun 3–6pm; mid-Dec to end Dec daily 3–7pm (Fri until 8pm).

Mountaineers' Cemetery ★★ CEMETERY   Take time out from the bustling main shopping street of Bahnhofstrasse to hunt down this small sliver of grassy land tucked just behind the Catholic Church of St. Mauritius. Zermatt has been a mecca for mountaineers ever since the dramatic first ascent of the Matterhorn by Edward Whymper in 1865, and many have lost their lives on this iconic peak and its surrounding

The World's Slowest Express Train

Zermatt is the start-point for one of the grandest and most scenic train rides in Europe. With daily departures, the **Glacier Express** ★★★ (www.glacierexpress.ch) might be the slowest express train in the world, taking 7½ hours to pass through southeastern Switzerland, but it's the most panoramic. A stunning feat of mountain engineering, the train crosses 291 bridges and goes through 91 tunnels as it snakes and loops its way through breath-taking landscapes, through entire mountains and over high alpine passes, arriving in the ritzy resort of St. Moritz in the canton of Graubünden around seven hours later. Windows on the train are designed to take in these stunning mountain panoramas. There's also a dining car on board. It's essential to book well in advance, by calling **Rail Europe** on © **800/622 86 00** (from the U.S.), or see their website at www.raileurope.com.

mountains. The cemetery contains the beautifully tended graves and memorials of a number of those heroic early mountaineers and mountain guides. One grave is poignantly marked *"Hier verloren wir das Leben, dort fanden wir es wieder. Auf dem heiligen Berg des Herrn."* ("We lost our lives here, but found them again there. On the holy mountain of the Lord.")

Behind the walls of the Church of St. Mauritius, off Kirchplatz. Free. Train (Zermatt).

St. Peter's Church ★ RELIGIOUS SITE The pretty, whitewashed Anglican St. Peter's Church, otherwise known as "The English Church," stands on a rocky ledge overlooking the village and holds a special place in Zermatt's history. During the golden age of alpinism, and the pioneering age of tourism, the majority of the visitors to the village came from England. Initially, Sunday services for English-speaking guests were held in the Monte Rosa and Mont Cervin hotels, but an increasing number of guests expressed the wish to have an Anglican church built. So St. Peter's was founded on donations from wealthy benefactors— some local, some English—including village hoteliers Alexander Seiler and Joseph Clemenz, and the relatives of Lord Douglas and Douglas Robert Hadow, two of the climbers who fell to their deaths during in the first ascent of the Matterhorn. The remains of a third victim, Reverend Charles Hudson, are buried under the high altar. Plaques inside the church recall other mountaineers associated with Zermatt. The church regularly holds services in English.

Just off the main street behind the Alpin Center. www.ics-uk. org/about-ics/seasonal-mission/st-peters-zermatt. ℂ **027/967 55 66.** Free. Train (Zermatt). Open hours vary.

Zermatt is a giant year-round recreation area for skiers and hikers. Since the first Swiss ski lessons were given here in 1902, it has ranked as one of the world's top ski resorts, offering skiing 365 days a year.

There are three main ski areas: Gornergrat, Rothorn, and Klein Matterhorn. The ski area also links up with Cervinia in Italy, although the best skiing is on the Swiss side. A variety of ski-lift passes are sold in various combinations, but there isn't much saving regardless of the plan you select. A day pass covering all the lifts in the Zermatt area (200km of piste) costs CHF79; while a 2-day pass is CHF146; add the Italian side (360km of piste) and it will cost you CHG170/CHF92 for 1 or 2 days. The one break that ski-pass holders do get is free rides on the ski bus linking all ski areas. To purchase tickets, book online at www.matterhornparadise.ch.

In summer, the high Alpine peaks encircling the resort offer some of Europe's finest hiking, and their way-marked treks are excellent for spotting alpine flora and fauna. Zermatt's Alpin Center (𝄋 **027/966 24 60**) offers year-round certified instruction and mountain guides for visitors wishing to explore Zermatt's mountains in summer and winter.

Gornergrat ★★★

The Gornergrat is accessed via a spectacular rack railroad, which departs from the village center and zig-zags its way up the mountain to the lofty altitude of 3,099m (10,165 ft.)—it is the highest open-air cogwheel railway in Europe. En route, you'll stop roughly half-way up at **Riffelberg,** which offers a panoramic view of both the Matterhorn and Mount Rosa. The complete ride from Zermatt to Gornergrat is CHF86 round-trip, or CHF43 one-way for ambitious skiers intending to return to the village on skis. At the summit, an observatory looks out on the bleak expanses of the Gorner glacier and over the heights of the Dom, which, at nearly 4,572m (14,996 ft.), is the highest mountain entirely within Switzerland. From here in summer, it is a gentle half-day's hike down past Riffelsee, where on a clear day you can see the Matterhorn perfectly reflected in the lake, to the hotel and restaurant at Riffelalp (see p. 139).

Blauherd-Unter Rothhorn ★★

To get to Blauherd-Unter Rothorn, take a cog railway through a tunnel from Zermatt to the alpine meadows of Sunegga, and then transfer to a cable car. After changing cable cars at Blauherd (which offers many hiking and skiing options of its own), you'll continue by cable car to the flat, rocky summit of the Unter Rothorn, where possibilities for alpine rambles or ski descents abound.

Schwarzsee-Theodul ★★

To reach Zermatt's third major ski area, take a cable car from Zermatt to **Furi-Schweigmatten** (usually abbreviated to Furi), or continue up by cable car to Schwarzsee (Black Lake) for sweeping vistas, more ski pistes and hiking trails and a sunny terrace for lunch and a drink at the **Hotel Schwarzsee** (ⓒ **0764/ 61 94 22**) at 2,584m (8,476 ft.). The round-trip excursion

from Zermatt to Schwarzsee costs CHF49. One of the most memorable hikes in the region is the climb up from Schwarzsee to the **Hörnli Hut** (3,260 m/10,700 ft.)—base-camp for the Matterhorn, just a few thousand feet below the wind-blasted cliffs that surround the summit.

Klein Matterhorn ★★★

To reach the "Little Matterhorn" from Furi, you must take two additional cable cars to Trocken-ersteg, and on to Klein Matterhorn—one of the highest mountain terraces in the world (3,760m/12,333 ft.). From the top, if the sky is clear, you can see the Swiss, French, and Italian Alps and breathe a rarefied air usually reserved for the hardiest of alpine climbers. There's downhill skiing here even in midsummer across the **Théodul Pass.** In winter, you can continue downhill on skis to the Italian ski resort of **Breuil-Cervinia** for lunch, on the opposite side of the Matterhorn from Zermatt. The excursion to Klein Matterhorn from Zermatt costs CHF99 round-trip.

133

Where to Stay

Zermatt has more than 120 hotels and guesthouses to suit all budgets, plus numerous private apartments and condominiums. Most hotels will meet you and your luggage at the cog-railway station by electric cart if you inform them in advance of your arrival time.

AROUND TOWN

Expensive

Hotel Monte Rosa ★★★ It can be hard to resist the opportunity to stay in Zermatt's first hotel. Named after Switzerland's highest mountain, the historic Monte Rosa originated as a simple wooden chalet in the earliest days of mountain tourism in 1839 (its guest list included Edward Whymper, the first man to summit the Matterhorn). Today's luxury historic hotel at the heart of the village was built on the original foundations in the 19th century. With its distinguished red-shuttered facade and exemplary standards, it seamlessly merges old-world atmosphere and nostalgia for days gone by with modern amenities. Tradition-steeped, timelessly elegant interiors draw a loyal clientele. No two rooms are the same—some are decorated with rich fabrics and antiques, while others have a more contemporary feel. Some of the deluxe suites boast Matterhorn views.

Bahnhofstrasse 80. www.monterosazermatt.ch. ✆ **027/966 03 33.** 41 units. Doubles CHF265–CHF860, suites CHF585–CHF2,320; rates include breakfast. Train (Zermatt). **Amenities:** Restaurant; cafe/bar; use of spa facilities in nearby hotel; ski room; free Wi-Fi.

The Omnia ★★★ Perched on a rock high above Zermatt, it's easy to feel at one with the elements here, thanks to the elevated location, a dramatic mountainous backdrop, and lower floors cut right into the rock. It's a bit like staying in the wilderness of the mountains, but with all the amenities at your doorstep—The Omnia is easily accessed via tunnel and lift from the village center. And that's not to mention the amazing views of Zermatt from the bedroom windows. The hotel describes itself as a "contemporary interpretation of the traditional mountain lodge"; to me, it's an upmarket, ultra-modern mountain retreat, with stylish on-trend designer fittings and a gorgeous indoor/outdoor infinity pool.

Auf dem Fels. www.the-omnia.com. © **027/966 71 71.** 30 units. Doubles CHF350–CHF3,500. Train (Zermatt). **Amenities:** Library; lounge bar; club/cinema; wellness center; meeting facilities; ski room; free Wi-Fi.

Moderate

Backstage Hotel ★★★ With its glass floors, floating fireplaces, and eccentric chandeliers made from musical instruments, this trailblazing, über-modern chalet hotel has won a clutch of design awards since its opening in 2010. Think high-tech interiors of walnut, velvet, distressed leather, and brushed stainless steel. For the ultimate design experience, request one of the six split-level, cube-shaped lofts when you book. In the basement, the entertainment space Vernissage contains an art gallery, cinema, and live-music venue. Guests can tuck into highly innovative Michelin-starred gourmet dining at the **After Seven** restaurant, but the real pièce de resistance of the property is the innovative wood, steel, and glass spa. A unique 3-hour experience is offered, comprising seven treatment "cubes" representing the seven days of creation, plus a host of special effects, including whale-song, live streaming from the Hubble Space

Telescope, and movement-sensitive music and video installations.

Hofmattstrasse 4. www.backstagehotel.ch. ☏ **027/966 69 70.** 19 units. Doubles CHF190–CHF210, cube lofts CHF390–CHF410; rates include breakfast and spa access. Train (Zermatt). **Amenities:** Restaurant; cafe; lounge-bar; sports shop; spa; Jacuzzi; cinema; art gallery; design shop; nightclub; ski room; free Wi-Fi.

Hotel Walliserhof ★★

Situated on Zermatt's car-free main street, this characterful, family-owned guesthouse is a charming place to stay. It's unmistakably Swiss with its elegant interiors, friendly staff dressed in traditional *Trachten,* and occasional Matterhorn glimpses from the balconies. Each room is different, although they are all essentially alpine-rustic, with pine-clad walls. The family rooms (some duplex) are practical and spacious. An ideal ski lodge, the walls are hung with wooden skis and vintage photos of mountaineers, and there's a well-heated ski room with boot warmers. There are two restaurants—the **Stübli** serves cheese specialties and rustic Swiss dishes (think röstis, fondues, and raclettes), while the **Restaurant Grill** serves a more international menu. The fitness room and mini wellness area in the basement offer a sauna, solarium, massage shower, steam room, and whirlpool access to soothe aching limbs.

Bahnhofstrasse 30. www.walliserhof-zermatt.ch. ☏ **027/966 65 55.** 34 units (including 4 family rooms). Doubles from CHF270, suites from CHF400; rates include breakfast and use of wellness area).Train (Zermatt). **Amenities:** 2 restaurants; smokers' lounge; fitness; wellness area; ski room; free Wi-Fi.

Romantik Hotel Julen ★★

Festooned with flowers in summer, this family-run hotel at the center of

Suite at Unique Hotel Post.

Zermatt is a stylish option all year-round. Behind the smart red shutters and ornate chalet exterior is a surprisingly bold, modern interior, with warm, strong colors and a cozy fireplace. Bedrooms offer a more traditional chalet ambiance, with spruce paneling and traditional light-pine furnishings. On top of a beautiful pool, sauna area, and caldarium, the spa and fitness center offers such unforgettable treats as indulgent après-ski massages and hay flower and goat-milk butter baths. Ask about the excellent ski packages, too.

Riedstrasse 2. www.julen.ch. ℰ **027/966 76 00.** 27 units. Doubles from CHF300–CHF600; rates include breakfast. Train (Zermatt). **Amenities:** 2 restaurants; 3 bars and clubs; spa; indoor swimming pool; fitness; ski room; free Wi-Fi.

Unique Hotel Post ★★★ This landmark hotel in the center of Zermatt has long appealed to the jet set for its stylish accommodation and après-ski scene. The hotel has been renovated in an extravagantly chic "mountain lodge style." Think smooth fir wood juxtaposed with exposed stone walls, and sleek lines softened with natural fabrics and furnishings in earthy tones. The spa offers sumptuous treatments in a serene environment. With its funky live music bar, pub, and legendary basement **Broken Bar Disco,** Hotel Post remains one of the hottest nightspots in town.

Bahnhofstrasse 41. www.hotelpost.ch. $\mathcal{C}$ **027/967 19 31.** 29 units. Doubles from CHF229, suites from CHF369; rates include breakfast and spa access. Train (Zermatt). **Amenities:** 4 restaurants; 5 bars and clubs; spa; ski room; free Wi-Fi.

Inexpensive

Hostel Matterhorn ★ Even by Swiss standards, Zermatt is a very expensive destination. Hostel Matterhorn provides a much-needed in-resort alternative; it's well-located, and although basic, it provides affordable accommodation for budget travelers. At the top of the village, close to the ski slopes, hiking, and biking trails, the hostel occupies a rustic timber chalet built in the '60s. Rooms are clean and no frills, but perfectly adequate, with shared bathroom facilities. Book in advance for weekends during the ski season, and bring your own sleeping bag.

Schluhmattstrasse 32. www.matterhornhostel.com. $\mathcal{C}$ **027/968 19 19.** 56 units plus 7 dormitory rooms. Dorm beds from CHF30, private rooms from CHF46. Train (Zermatt). **Amenities:** Bar and restaurant; lounge; in-room lockers; ski room; free Wi-Fi.

Hotel Daniela ★★ Hotel Daniela holds down a secluded location away from the bustle of the village center, but within easy walking distance of all the shops and boutiques. It's a modern property, built in the classic chalet style. The interior is traditional and elegant, with beautiful, vibrant furnishings and well-appointed bedrooms. Rooms on the third floor have views across village rooftops to the Matterhorn, and the spacious family rooms are especially good values. The Daniela is a sister hotel to the **Romantik Hotel Julen ★★** (they share the same management; see listing above), so guests can enjoy the peace and quiet (and smaller price tag) of these more modest accommodations, yet still have access to the spa, swimming pool, and fine dining of the more deluxe sibling just a stone's throw away. Steinmattstrasse 39. www.julen.ch/en/hotel-daniela. © **027/ 966 77 00.** 24 units. Doubles CHF120–CHF350. Train (Zermatt). **Amenities:** Breakfast area; restaurant and spa in nearby hotel; ski room; free Wi-Fi.

IN THE MOUNTAINS

Expensive

Riffelalp Resort ★★★ A 20-minute uphill ride through breathtaking scenery on the Gornergrat cogwheel train brings guests to the Riffelalp plateau where a private tram (summer months only) leads through fragrant pine forests to this deluxe five-star mountain resort, face-to-face with the mighty Matterhorn. A ski-in ski-out hotel in winter and a trekker's paradise in summer, this beautiful mountain oasis boasts cozy, wood-clad guest rooms with classic furnishings, a sumptuous spa, and Europe's highest outdoor swimming pool. Dining options range from haute cuisine in Restaurant Alexandre to tasty fondues and raclettes at the traditional Walliser-Keller in winter. The hotel's certified ski instructor and mountain guide offers a winter program of skiing, snowshoeing, heliskiing, Velogemel, tobogganing, and glacier skiing. At 2,222m (7,290 ft.), this is definitely a place where you can enjoy the high life.

Riffelalp Plateau. www.riffelalp.com. © **027/699 05 55.** 72 units. Doubles CHF430–CHF1,200 suites CHF715–CHF2,570; rates include half-board and train fares between Zermatt and Riffelalp. Train (Zermatt) then Gornergrat Railway. **Amenities:** 2 restaurants; bar; smokers' lounge; spa; swimming pool; wine shop; gym; ski instructor/mountain guide; ice skating; tennis court; ski room; free Wi-Fi.

Moderate

Iglu-dorf ★★   For the ultimate romantic experience, stay in one of the highest igloos in the world. "Igloo Village" holds down a spot way up on the mountainside near the Matterhorn at an altitude of 2,727m (8,947 ft.). The full package here includes mulled wine, cheese fondue, a hot tub, nighttime snowshoeing, an ice bar, breakfast in a mountain restaurant, and sleeping bags and liners suitable for as low as -40°C. The range of accommodation goes from special "romantic" igloos for honeymooning couples (with spacious facilities, breathtaking views, and plenty of Prosecco) to the more basic "standard igloo" that sleeps up to six and is ideal for adventurous families. The igloo season runs approximately Christmas to mid-April, depending on snow conditions. Make sure you bring plenty of warm, winter-proof clothing and cash—credit cards are not accepted. There is no Wi-Fi.

Gornergrat. www.iglu-dorf.com. ✆ **041/612 27 28.** 11 units. Package price per person CHF159–CHF499. Train (Zermatt) then Gornergrat railway to Gornergrat. **Amenities:** Hot tub; ice bar.

Where to Eat

You'll be spoiled for choice of eatery in Zermatt, with its many excellent restaurants serving traditional Swiss dishes and Continental cuisine. Most of the best restaurants are connected with hotels and, given the well-heeled traveler who tends to come to this resort, none of them will hesitate to separate you from your money.

Enjoying fondu at the Iglu-dorf.

AROUND TOWN
Expensive
Capri ★★ ITALIAN   This Michelin-starred gourmet Italian restaurant right on the Italo-Swiss border is the jewel in the culinary crown of the beautiful five-star Mont Cervin Palace Hotel, serving classic Italian dishes with a contemporary twist. Situated on the fourth floor, the space is accompanied by views of the Matterhorn in an elegant, if unremarkable, dining room. Capri has a reputation as the best Italian restaurant in Switzerland, so advanced booking is essential. Mont Cervin Palace Hotel, Bahnhofstrasse 31. www.montcervin palace.ch/en. © **027/966 88 88.** Mains CHF50–CHF60. Train (Zermatt). Late Dec to early Apr, Tues–Sun 7–11pm.

Cervo ★★ SWISS Part of the boutique Hotel Cervo, the main appeal here is simplicity. Chef Seraina Lauber takes traditional Swiss recipes and reinvigorates them, using the freshest seasonal ingredients, many of which have been grown in the chalet's own vegetable garden, to create a perfect blend of old and new. Try caramelized cheese on a beetroot and leaf salad with smoked pecans; then the black cod with white pine needles, elderflowers, and black rice; followed by meringues and pickled apricots and almonds with lavender cream; or an array of homemade ice creams and sorbets. Combine those scrumptious dishes with crisp, modern-rustic decor and a reliable selection of fine local wines, and you will be guaranteed a meal to remember. Reservations are recommended.

Hotel Cervo, Riedweg 156. www.cervo.ch. © **027/968 12 12.** Mains CHF42–CHF72. Train (Zermatt). Dec to late Apr daily noon–10pm.

Elsie's Bar ★ OYSTERS Elsie's Bar is where the jet set head at the end of a hard day's skiing to tuck into platters of shucked oysters, washed down with the finest of champagnes. Elsie's oozes tradition and old-world charm, from its cozy wooden interiors to the old-fashioned paintings of Zermatt on its walls. In the '60s it was known for its snails and Irish coffees, in the '70s for its ham and eggs with Berlin-style pancakes. Today it serves a small selection of upmarket delicacies—caviar, snails, oysters, homemade *foie gras,* and beef tartar—along with an outstanding menu of whiskeys and wines.

Kirchplatz 16. www.elsiebar.ch. © **027 967 24 31.** Mains CHF46–CHF68. Train (Zermatt). Mid-Nov to Apr daily 4pm–2am; June to mid-Oct, Mon–Sat 2:30pm–midnight, Sun 4–10pm.

MEALS IN THE mountains

Zermatt boasts some excellent mountaintop restaurants, feeding the many hikers, skiers, and mountain-bikers who pass by. High upon a glacier, **Bergrestaurant Fluhalp** ★★ (www.fluhalp-zermatt.ch; ✆ **027/967 25 97**) is the perfect place to go for a leisurely lunch in the sunshine way up on the Rothorn, with unparalleled Matterhorn vistas. The menu comprises delicious soups, pastas, röstis, fondues, copious salads, and steaks, all at reasonable prices. **Restaurant Alexandre** ★ offers gourmet Swiss cuisine with an impressive wine list atop the Riffelalp (see p. 139). But our favorite mountain haunt is the quaint **Bergrestaurant Blatten** ★★★ (www.blatten-zermatt.ch; ✆ **027/967 20 96**), one of Zermatt's oldest eateries, nestled above the ancient wooden hamlet of Blatten, with its unbeatable alpine cuisine (try the glistening fruit tarts and homemade ice creams) accompanied by jaw-dropping views from the sun terrace.

Le Gitan ★★ INTERNATIONAL There's something rather special about Le Gitan. Perhaps it's the chef preparing roasted meats before your eyes, over a wood fire right in the middle of the candlelit dining room. Maybe it's the cozy, old-fashioned cafe at the front, a perfect place to chill and unwind after an exhilarating day in the mountains. Or it could be the stylish bar, standing by to round off a perfect evening with a classic cocktail. One thing is for certain, this popular, family-run restaurant offers a warm and friendly welcome and delicious, memorable alpine cuisine. Book in advance to avoid disappointment.
Hotel Darioli, Bahnhofstrasse 64. www.legitan.ch. ✆ **027/968 19 40.** Mains CHF49–CHF88. Train (Zermatt). Daily noon–2pm, 6:30pm–midnight (kitchen closes at 9:30pm).

Moderate

Stockhorn Grill ★★ SWISS   This classic restaurant is something of a local institution. It serves a host of traditional Swiss fare, but the real specialties here are the mouth-wateringly tender grilled meats, cooked over a wood fire. Other staples include the ubiquitous Swiss-cheese fondue, regional raclette and meat fondues, all served in a cozy wood-clad interior, or on the terrace in summer. The restaurant is part of the Hotel Stockhorn, which belongs to the family of the legendary Matterhorn guide Emil Julen, and is hugely popular with both locals and visitors.

Hotel Stockhorn, Riedstrasse. www.grill-stockhorn.ch. © **027/ 967 17 47.** Mains from CHF27. Train (Zermatt). Tues–Sun, 6:30pm–midnight; closed mid-May to mid-June and mid-Oct to mid-Nov.

Inexpensive

Whymper-Stube ★★ SWISS   Of Zermatt's numerous fondue joints, our favorite is the Whymper-Stube on the lower level of the legendary Hotel Monte Rosa. Perhaps it's for the historic connection—Englishman Edward Whymper allegedly plotted the first ascent of the Matterhorn here in 1865—or perhaps it's simply because you'll find here some of the town's tastiest fondues and raclette. There are meat fondues; and several different types of gooey cheese fondue, including the option to have all three types at once for those who can't decide. The snug dining room is appropriately rustic, with its stone floor, candles, and age-darkened wood-paneled walls.

Hotel Monte Rosa, Bahnhofstrasse 80. www.whymper-stube. ch. © **027/967 22 96.** Raclette CHF9 per person, fondues CHF25–CHF44 and up. Train (Zermatt). Daily 11am–midnight.

Shopping

Zermatt's critics accuse it of combining a hard-nosed commercialism, shrewdly calculating the value of every snowflake, with a less harsh obsession with Swiss folklore. Consequently, the town's main shopping thoroughfare, **Bahnhofstrasse,** contains branches of stores you might have expected only in much larger cities, with an emphasis on luxury goods, alpine souvenirs, and sporting goods. Ski and mountaineering equipment here tends to be state of the art; sports stores abound, but one worthwhile example is **Slalom Sport,** Kirchstrasse 17 (www.slalom-sport.ch; ℂ 027/966-23-66), close to the village church. Well-recommended competitors, both on Bahnhofstrasse near the Gornergrat cable car, include **Glacier Sport** (ℂ 027/967-27-19) and **Bayard Sport** (www.bayard zermatt.ch; ℂ 027/966-49-50).

Local souvenirs in Zermatt include everything from the genuinely artful to the hopelessly kitschy. One such outlet is **WEGA,** on Bahnhofplatz (www.wega-zermatt.ch; ℂ 027/967-21-66). The cakes, pastries, and mini chocolate Matterhorns at **Fuchs** (Getwingstrasse 24; www.fuchs-zermatt.ch; ℂ 027/967-20-63) are hard to resist.

Snow and ice aren't the only things that sparkle in glitzy Zermatt, so if you're susceptible to impulse purchases of jewelry, one of the best places to browse is **Bijouterie Schindler** (Bahnhofstrasse 5; ℂ 027/967-11-18), which stockpiles both Swiss watches and gemstones.

The charming town of Furi near Zermatt.

Entertainment & Nightlife

This glamorous resort has been a favorite destination of the jet set for decades, so it's little surprise that Zermatt is as strong on après-ski activities—which include tea dances, bars, nightclubs, and discos—as it is on skiing. It starts with *glühwein* (hot mulled wine) in the slopeside bars and restaurants at **Furi, Blatten,** and **Zum See,** then spills into the bars en route down to Zermatt, including the eternally popular **Hennu Stall,** the terrace bar of **Hotel Cervo,** the **Zermatt Yacht Club,** and **Snowboat.** Other choice venues include any number of tearooms, the legendary **Elsie's Bar** (see p. 142), or **Little Bar** and **Hexenbar** on the main drag.

After dark, **Hotel Post** (www.hotelpost.ch; 𝄒 **027/967-19-31;** see p. 137), where everybody shows up after recovering from Elsie's Irish coffee, has a virtual monopoly on nightlife in Zermatt. The owner, Karl Ivarsson, an American, has gradually expanded it into one of the most complete entertainment complexes in Zermatt, with a number of restaurants and nightspots under one roof: choose from the **Pink Live Music Bar** for live jazz and soul music (open Dec–Easter); the rustic **Brown Cow** for those with hunger pangs (the menu includes hamburgers, salads, and sandwiches); or join ski bums in the basement **Broken Bar** for some more vigorous partying. Other highly animated venues include **Papperla Pub** (www.papperlapub.ch; 𝄒 **027/967-40-40**) and **GramPi's** in Bahnhofstrasse (www.grampis.ch; 𝄒 **027/967-77-88**), frequented by the resort's army of seasonaires and ski instructors.

Entertainment & Nightlife

ZERMATT

Other less obvious venues include the ultra-hip **Vernissage Bar** in Backstage Hotel (www.backstage-hotel.ch; ✆ **027/966-69-70;** see p. 135) with its art gallery, cinema and live music venue; and the **Kegelstube ("Bowling Alley Bar")** in Hotel Bristol (✆ **027/966-33-80**), which contains the resort's only bowling alley.

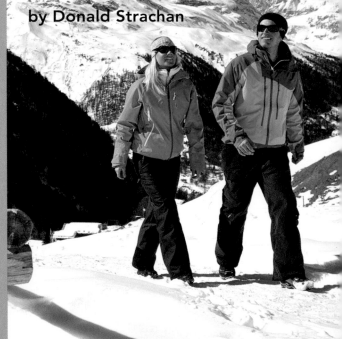

PLANNING
YOUR TRIP

by Donald Strachan

A little planning goes a long way, especially when you are traveling to and through a country with several different languages, transport systems, airlines, festivals, and sights to see. This chapter provides a variety of invaluable aids, including information on how to get there from the U.S. and Canada, the U.K., and Australia or New Zealand; the most efficient and budget-friendly ways of getting around; tips on where to stay; and quick, on-the-ground resources for savvy travel around Switzerland.

GETTING THERE
By Plane

The key factor determining what you'll pay is **season:** Tickets tend to be cheaper if you fly off season. **High season** on most routes is usually from June to mid-September and December through February—the most expensive and most crowded time to travel. **Shoulder season** is from April to May and mid-September to October. **Low season**— usually with the cheapest fares and regular aggressive offers—is in November and March. You can sometimes save money by flying midweek, too, or by spending at least a Saturday night in your destination.

Begin thinking about flying plans at least 6 months ahead of time. Consider exchange rate movements: Fares may be calculated in U.S. dollars, British pounds, or euros, depending on the airline. The key window for finding a **deal** is usually between 5 and 6 months ahead of your departure according to a massive study of some 21 million fare transactions by the Airline Reporting Corporation (a middleman between travel agencies and the airlines). They also found that those who booked on a Sunday statistically found the best rates (on average they paid 19% less than those who booked midweek).

The glory days of generous **frequent flyer programs** and bucketloads of free miles are no more, but those who collect miles via credit cards (rather than trying to fly to get them) are having better luck getting free trips nowadays. The key strategy is to get a card that will work with a number of airlines, rather than one branded by a particular airline (as those usually have less generous rates of return and more draconian fees). The forum **Flyertalk.com** is a handy resource for learning how to get the most out of your miles (both for airlines and hotels); such companies as AwardMagic.com and IFlyWithMiles.com can help stressed travelers redeem miles for flights for a flat fee that's usually far less than a ticket from the United States to Europe would have cost.

If you're not using miles, remember that the cheapest way between two points may not always be a straight line. Such newish airlines as **XL, WOW Airlines,** and **Norwegian** have been offering particularly good values for travel from the United States to Europe. Run searches through the regular online agents such as Expedia, as well as metasearch engines like **DoHop.com, Kayak.com, Skyscanner.net,** and **Momondo.com.** For complex journeys, with multiple departures, doing multiple searches (so such affordable intra-European airlines Germanwings, EasyJet and Ryanair show up on the search) is a good way to find deals; a specialist flight agent such as **RoundtheWorldFlights.com** or **AirTreks.com** will also likely save you money.

GETTING AROUND
By Train

In Switzerland, the shortest—and often cheapest—distance between two points is usually lined with rail tracks. Compared to the United States, for example, Swiss trains are less expensive, far more advanced in many ways, and the rail systems are certainly more extensive. Although it doesn't rival modern Asian rail networks such as Japan's, the Swiss rail system still ranks as one of the best in the world:

Modern **high-speed trains** (traveling up to around 180 mph) make the rails faster than the plane for short.

SOME IMPORTANT TRAIN NOTES

Many Swiss high-speed trains require you to pay a **supplement** in addition to the regular ticket fare. It's included when you buy tickets, but not usually in any prepaid rail pass, so check at the ticket window before boarding; otherwise, the conductor will sell you the supplement on the train—along with a fine. **Seat reservations** (from 10€ up) are required on some high-speed runs, too. You can usually reserve a seat within a few hours of departure, but be on the safe side and book your seat a few days in advance for any key connections you're building into an itinerary. You need to reserve any sleeping couchette or sleeping berth too.

With some exceptions, there's usually no need to buy individual train tickets or make seat reservations many months before you leave home.

The difference between **first class** and **second class** on European trains is often minor—a matter of 1 or 2 inches of extra padding and maybe a bit more elbowroom. However, upgrades can sometimes be fairly cheap. There's sometimes a complimentary snack thrown in, along with free Wi-Fi. So, our general advice is: Upgrade if it doesn't cost very much to do so, but don't break the bank.

European **train stations** are usually as clean and efficient as the trains, if a bit chaotic at times. In stations you'll find departures boards showing the track number and timetables for regularly scheduled runs (departures are sometimes on a yellow poster, too). Many stations also have tourist offices, banks with ATMs, and newsstands where you can buy phone cards, bus and metro tickets, maps, and local English-language event magazines. Some have shopping malls and hotels, or even public showers.

You can get more details about train travel in Europe by contacting **Rail Europe** (www.raileurope. com; also ☎ **0871/231-0790** in the U.K.) Other excellent agents worth consulting for planning assistance and advance ticket or pass sales include **International Rail** (www.internationalrail.com; ☎ **0871/ 231-0790** in the U.K.) and **TrainsEurope** (www. trainseurope.co.uk; ☎ **0871/700-7722** in the U.K.). Note that schedules are confirmed and tickets released between 60 and 90 days from travel dates. The most valuable bookmark for planning complex European rail journeys is **The Man in Seat Sixty-One** (www. seat61.com). It also now has a booking engine for train travel.

TRAIN trip tips

To make your train travels as pleasant as possible, remember a few general rules:

o **Hold on to your train ticket** after it's been marked or punched by the conductor. Some European rail networks require that you present your ticket when you leave the station platform at your destination.

o While you sleep—or even nap—**be sure your valuables are in a safe place.** You might temporarily attach a small bell to each bag to warn you if someone attempts to take it. If you've left bags on a rack in the front or back of the car, consider securing them with a small bicycle chain and lock to deter thieves, who consider trains happy hunting grounds.

o Few European trains have drinking fountains, and the dining car may be closed just when you're at your thirstiest, so **take along a bottle of mineral water.** As you'll soon discover, the experienced rail traveler comes loaded with hampers of food and drink and munches away throughout the trip—buying food onboard can be very expensive.

o If you want to leave bags in a train station locker, **don't let anyone help you store them in it.** An old trick among thieves is feigned helpfulness, and then pocketing the key to your locker while passing you the key to an empty one.

By Car

Most rental companies offer their best prices to customers who **reserve in advance** from their home country. Weekly rentals are almost always less expensive than day rentals. Three or more people traveling

the rules of the road:
DRIVING IN EUROPE

- First, know that European drivers tend to be more **aggressive** than their counterparts from other parts of the world.

- **Drive on the right** except in England, Scotland, and Ireland, where you drive on the left. And *do not drive* in the left lane on a four-lane highway; it is only for passing.

- If someone comes up from behind and flashes his lights at you, it's a signal for you to slow down and either move to the right lane or drive more on the shoulder so that he can pass you more easily (two-lane roads here sometimes become three cars wide).

- Except for the German Autobahn, most highways

- do indeed have **speed limits** of around 100 to 130kmph (62–81 mph).

- Remember that outside the U.K., everything's measured in **kilometers** (distance and speed limits). For a rough conversion, 1km = 0.6 miles.

- Be aware that fuel is *very* expensive, so you should **rent the smallest, most fuel-efficient car** you think you can manage. Prices at the pumps are quoted in liters (1 U.S. gallon = 3.78 liters).

- Never leave anything of value in a car overnight, and don't leave anything visible when you leave the car.

together can often get around cheaper by car than by train, depending on the distances traveled and the size and efficiency of the engine—compared to most other parts of the world, fuel is very expensive almost everywhere in Europe. You should also factor in **road tolls** that many countries charge. Also keep in mind that the vast majority of available rental cars have **manual transmissions** (stick shifts). Automatics are available, but for a premium.

When you reserve a car, be sure to ask if the price includes: all taxes including value-added tax (VAT); breakdown assistance; unlimited mileage; personal accident or liability insurance (PAI); collision-damage waiver (CDW); theft waiver; and any other insurance options. If not, ask what these extras cost, because they can make a big dent in your bottom line. The CDW and other insurance might be covered by your credit card if you use the card to pay for the rental; check with your card issuer to be sure. Some travelers like to live dangerously and waive optional insurance. But when no CDW is purchased, many rental agencies will make you pay for any damages on the spot when you return the car—making even the smallest dent or scratch a potentially costly experience. To avoid any issues, take cellphone photos of your car with a time stamp, so that you have any dents and dings recorded and won't be charged for them.

If your credit card doesn't cover the CDW, consider buying Car Rental Collision Coverage from a third party. **Travel Guard** (www.travelguard.com; ✆ **800/826-1300** in the U.S. and Canada), which will insure you for around US$7 to US$9 per day. In the U.K., **Insurance 4 Car Hire** (www.insurance 4carhire.com; ✆ **0844/892-1770**) offers similar cover. An annual policy covering unlimited car rental for a maximum of 31 consecutive days on any one trip costs £49. That being said, these are just two players and others may have better rates. To see side-by-side comparisons of CDW rentals, go to the marketplace site www.tripinsurancestore.com.

IMPORTANT rental-car **TIPS**

Check what type of fuel your car takes: If you damage the car's engine by pumping gasoline rather than diesel, most European car insurance policies won't protect you.

Choose a smart size for your car: In many of Switzerland's villages, the streets were formed well before cars were invented. So having too large a car can limit where you can drive.

Pack light: Even the larger European cars will have smaller trunks than we're used to in the United States. If you must bring a large suitcase, inquire whether your car will have a roof rack.

Take two credit cards: Often, rental companies will freeze and amount equal to the CDW coverage

deductible on the credit card that you use to rent the car. So you're going to want to have a second card handy so that you don't go over your limit with the first.

See if there are any special regulations for the country you're visiting: This is particularly important if you're crossing borders in your rental car. In Italy, for example, it's the law that you must buy insurance through your rental company; credit card insurance isn't accepted on the Boot.

Don't rent a car for city stays: Every city in Switzerland, every single one, has terrific public transportation options. You'll ONLY need a car if you're traveling in the Swiss countryside. Having a car in a Swiss city is usually an expensive hassle.

The main international companies all have rental points across Europe: **Avis** (www.avis.com; © **800/ 633-3469** in the U.S. and **800/879-2847** in Canada), **Budget** (www.budget.com; © **800/218-7992** in the U.S. and **800/268-8900** in Canada), **Dollar** (www.dollar.com; 🕿 **800/800-5252** in the U.S. and Canada), **Hertz** (www.hertz.com; 🕿 **800/654-3131** in the U.S. and Canada), and **National** (www.national car.com; 🕿 **877/222-9058** in the U.S. and Canada). U.S.-based companies specializing in European rentals include **Auto Europe** (www.autoeurope.com; 🕿 **888/223-5555** in the U.S. and Canada), **Europcar** (www.europcar.com), **Europe by Car** (www.europe bycar.com; 🕿 **800/223-1516** in the U.S. and Canada), **Kemwel** (www.kemwel.com; 🕿 **877/820-0668** in the U.S. and Canada) and **Sixt** (www.sixt. com). It's also worth checking prices offered by U.K.–based rental agents such as **Holiday Autos** (www. holidayautos.co.uk; 🕿 **44/203-740-9859** in the U.K.). Europe by Car, Kemwel, and **Renault USA** (www. renaultusa.com; 🕿 **888/532-1221** in the U.S. and Canada) also offer a competitive alternative to renting for longer than 15 days: **short-term leases** in which you technically buy a fresh-from-the-factory car and then sell it back when you return it. All insurance is included, from liability and theft to personal injury and CDW, with no deductible. And unlike at many rental agencies, who won't rent to anyone 24 and under, the minimum age for a lease is 18. You should also always check your quote against quotes from general travel search sites like **Kayak.com**, as well as car-rental search specialists such as **RhinoCarHire.com** and **CarHireSearch.co.uk**.

For visitors coming from North America, the **AAA** supplies good maps to its members. **Michelin maps** (www.viamichelin.co.uk) are made with the tourist in mind, and are widely available in shops and fuel stations across Switzerland. There's also a handy route planner online. Be aware that, if you are planning to navigate using your mobile phone, data costs for roaming can be very expensive.

By Bus

Bus transportation is readily available throughout Switzerland; it often is less expensive than train travel and covers a more extensive area, but is slower and can be much less comfortable. European buses, like the trains, outshine their American counterparts, but they're perhaps best used only to pick up where the extensive train network leaves off. One major long-haul bus company serves almost all the countries of western, northern, and eastern Europe: **Eurolines** (www.eurolines.com; ✆ **0871/781-8178** in the U.K., **0861/1991 900** in Italy, **6196/2078-501** in Germany). The staff at Eurolines can check schedules, make reservations, and quote prices for travel between cities Europe-wide.

WHEN TO GO

Change this graf to: The high season lasts from mid-May to mid-September and also encompasses ski season from December through February. These are the most expensive times to go to Switzerland.

You'll find smaller crowds, relatively fair weather, and often lower prices at hotels in the **shoulder seasons,** from Easter to mid-May and mid-September to October. **Off season** (except at ski resorts) is from November to Easter, with the exception of the Christmas period. While prices plunge in the city in low season, tourist facilities in some smaller towns shut down altogether, so do advance research if you're planning on going out into the Swiss countryside during the late-fall, early spring, and winter months. Much of Europe, takes August off, and August 15 to August 30 is vacation time for many locals, so expect the cities to be devoid of natives and many restaurants and shops to be closed—but the beaches and lakes packed.

Weather

The Alpine climate means winters are cold and bright, and spring comes late, with snow falls well into April. Summers are mild and sunny, with delightfully fresh air, though the alpine regions can experience dramatic changes in weather any time of year. Summer storms aren't uncommon.

TIPS ON WHERE TO STAY

Traditional European hotels tend to be **simpler** than North American ones, and rooms are on average significantly **smaller.** Hoteliers tend to emphasize character and friendliness over amenities. For example, even in the cheapest American chain motel, free cable is as standard as indoor plumbing. In Europe, however, some independent hotels below the moderate level don't even have in-room TVs. But then, you're probably not over here to watch *The X-Factor*.

Make advance reservations for the popular months of travel. Travel to most places in Europe peaks between May and October, and during that period, it's hard to come by a moderate or inexpensive hotel room. And many smaller, boutique hotels can fill up year-round, especially at weekends and in popular city-break or weekend bolthole destinations. For off-season, you'll often find the best lodging deals by waiting until the last minute, particularly if you use the web. Such websites as **Priceline.com** and **Hotwire.com** can be gold for last-minute deals, as can the popular app **HotelTonight** (which books weeklong stays, despite the name, but only at the last minute).

You'll find hotels and other accommodations inside every conceivable kind of building, from 21st-century concrete cubes to medieval coaching inns. In older hotels, guest rooms can be smaller than you might expect (if you base your expectation on a modern U.S. Radisson, for example), and each room is usually different, sometimes quirkily so. But this is part of the charm. Some rooms may only have a shower, not a bathtub, so if you feel you can't survive without a tub, make that clear when booking.

Most European countries rate hotels by **stars,** ranging from five stars (luxe) to one star (modest). A four- or five-star hotel offers first-class accommodations, a three-star hotel is usually moderately priced, and a one- or two-star hotel is inexpensively priced. Governments grant stars based on rigid, often bizarre, criteria, evaluating such amenities as elevators, private bathrooms, pools, and air-conditioning. The hotel with the most stars is not necessarily the most elegant or charming. For example, a five-star hotel might be an ugly, modern building, whereas a one-star hotel might be a townhouse but with no elevator, bar, or restaurant. Plenty of fashionable boutique accommodations have no stars at all. Unless otherwise noted, all hotel rooms in this book have **private en suite bathrooms.** And the stars you'll see in this book are based on the assessments of our authors, not on the government criteria. We have no "no" star hotels. Instead, a one-star is a place we think gives good value for the money, a two-star is highly recommended, and a three-star property would be appropriate for a honeymoon or some other type of special-event travel. It will be a very unique and wonderful place (and we're proud to say, some of our three-star properties are budget ones).

You probably don't want to stay in a chain hotel (unless you're trying to help your budget by using hotel award points). If that's the case, know that you'll find all of the large, multinational chains in Europe's capitals, and they'll usually be well-maintained and well-located. For car-tourers, **Ibis** (www.ibishotel.com) are reliable, clean, well-equipped, and value overnight motel-style stops close to many major highways. There are over 700 in Europe. In fact, Ibis's parent **Accor** group (www.accorhotels.com) has hotel offerings at just about every level of comfort in several European countries—brands include Mercure, Sofitel, and Novotel. **Louvre Hotels** (www.louvrehotels.com) has a number of affordable brands, including Campanile. Reliable, midrange brands and chains like **Best Western** (www.bestwestern.com) and **Holiday Inn** (www.holidayinn.com) are here too. **Radisson Blu** (www.radissonblu.com) has a strong presence in Europe's cities. You'll find our favorite hotels by consulting the individual chapters in this book.

A **villa** or **rental property** can be great for getting up-close to a European destination, if you're lingering in one spot for more than a couple of nights. **Untours** (www.untours.com; © **888/868-6871** in the U.S. and Canada) provides apartment, farmhouse, or cottage stays of 2 weeks or more in many destinations for a reasonable price, and with the on-the-ground support of a host. **HomeAway.com** is the largest rental property broker on the planet, and offers properties of every kind all over Europe. It owns VRBO. com, which has a similarly wide array of villas and apartments. Other large web-based rental specialists include **FlipKey.com** and **Rentalo.com**. **Holiday lettings.co.uk** and **Homelidays** (www.homelidays. co.uk) both have vast rental property portfolios, including villas with private or shared outdoor pools.

HomeLink International (www.homelink.org; ☎ **800/638-3841** in the U.S, or ☎ **01962/886882** in the U.K.), which costs $119/£115 for a year's membership, is the oldest, largest, and best home-exchange holiday group in the world. An alternative is is **Intervac International** (www.intervac-homeexchange.com; ☎ **866/844-7567** in the U.S., ☎ **353-41-9837969** in the U.K.), which costs $100 annually. Both have members spread around Europe.

Many Swiss cities are also well represented in online peer-to-peer accommodation networks, including international giants like **AirBnB.com**; **9flats. com** and **Wimdu.com** are other peer-to-peer site worth checking out.

ORGANIZED TOURS

Active Tours

CYCLING

Cycling tours are a great way to see Switzerland—if you have the stamina. But avid bikers love the challenge of the Alps, making biking tours to this hilly region quite popular. **Bike Switzerland** (www.

HIKING & WALKING

Wilderness Travel (www.wildernesstravel.com; ☎ **800/ 368-2794** or 510/558-2488 in the U.S. and Canada), specializes in walking tours, treks, and inn-to-inn hiking tours of almost 20 European countries, as well as less strenuous walking tours. **Sherpa Expeditions** (www.sherpaexpeditions.com; © **020/8577-2717** in the U.K.), offers both self-guided and group treks through off-the-beaten-track regions. Two somewhat upscale walking-tour companies are **Butterfield & Robinson** (www.butterfield.com; © **866/551-9090** in the U.S. and Canada); and **Country Walkers** (www.countrywalkers.com; © **800/234-6900** in the U.S. and Canada, or 1300/663-206 in Australia). **Macs Adventure** (www.macsadventure.com; © **844/ 896-6799** in the U.S. and Canada, © **0141/530- 3712** in the U.K.) has an impressive portfolio of serviced active holidays, with a number of adventures in the Mont Blanc area. **Exodus** (www.exodus.co.uk; © **0845/287-3789** in the U.K.) has walks and hikes for all ability levels including ice treks in winter.

One of the best companies is **Equitour** (www. ridingtours.com; © **800/545-0019** or 307/455-3363 in the U.S. and Canada), which offers 5- to 7-day rides through many of Europe's most beautiful areas, such as the Scottish Highlands and France's Loire Valley. **FlorenceTown** (www.florencetown.com; © **055/ 281-103** in Italy) runs easy 1-day rides around the Chianti region of Tuscany.

Nature Tours

Butterflies and alpine flowers are the focus of trips from **Naturetrek** (www.naturetrek.co.uk; © **01962/ 733-051** in the U.K.), whose naturalists lead walks through some of the Switzerland's most spectacular scenery.

Escorted General-Interest Tours

Escorted tours are structured group tours, with a group leader. The price usually includes everything from airfare to hotels, meals, tours, admission costs, and local transportation. Group tours are best for people who want to have the company of other travelers as they tour about and who are nervous about planning their own itinerary. They will not save you money on travel, nor do they offer experiences that most travelers, with this book in hand, can't replicate on their own. That includes guided tours, which can be picked up, on a day-trip basis, in every tourist destination in Europe. But if you want the social aspects of a tour, we highly recommend that you get one that does NOT include meals, as you'll eat much better, and eating well is an integral part of the European experience. With a group tour, you'll be dining at the places that can handle 40 people emerging from a bus all at once (meaning the places the locals have long ago abandoned).

The two largest tour operators conducting escorted tours of Europe are various brands under the umbrella of **Globus/Cosmos** (www.globusandcosmos.com; ✆ **866/755-8581** in the U.S. and Canada, or ✆ **0800/223-0179** in the U.K.) and **Trafalgar** (www.trafalgartours.com; ✆ **0800/533-5619** in the U.K.). Both have tours in all price ranges, the differences consisting of hotel location and the number of activities. (With the cheaper tours, you'll often find yourself stuck out in a suburban hotel, rather than near to sights and restaurants you might want to explore on your own.) There's little difference in the companies' services, so choose your tour based on the itinerary and preferred date of departure. Brochures are available at travel agencies, and there's plenty of itinerary information and ideas online. Other well-respected group tour operators include **GoAhead Tours** (www.goaheadtours.com; ☎ **877/264-1348**); ☎ **800/431-1515**); **Gate 1 Travel** (www.gate1travel.com; ☎ **800/682-3333**); and **YMT Vacations** (www.ymtvacations.com; ☎ **855/804-4725**).

Packages for Independent Travelers

Package tours are simply a way to buy the airfare, accommodations, and other elements of your trip (such as car rentals, airport transfers, and sometimes even activities) at the same time and often at discounted prices.

All major airlines flying from North America to Europe sell vacation packages, but the price-leaders is such specialists as **GoToday** (www.gotoday.com; ☎ **800/227-3235**). Several big **online travel agencies**—Expedia, Travelocity, Orbitz, and Lastminute.com—also do a brisk business in packages for visitors flying from just about anywhere to pretty much anywhere else. Pretty much every European short-haul airline these days—including British Airways, Ryanair, and others—offers flight plus hotel plus car rental deals. Keep an eye on their websites.

For all kinds of packages with a sustainable or eco-friendly ethos, check the listings at **Responsible Travel** (www.responsibletravel.com or www.responsiblevacation.com).

Deals on packages come and go, and the latest are often listed at Frommers.com, so please do search our "Deals" section.

[FastFACTS] EUROPE

Business Hours

Bank hours vary but are generally Monday to Friday, 8:30am to 4:30pm (closed on public holidays). Most **shops** are open Monday to Friday from 8am to 6:30pm, and on Saturday from 8am to 4pm; in cities, some of the large stores stay open until 9pm on Thursdays.

Car Rental

See "Getting Around by Car," earlier in this chapter.

Cellphones

See "Mobile Phones," later in this section.

Currency

Perpetually neutral and independent Switzerland is not a member of the European Union and as such, uses its own currency, the Swiss franc (CHF). Still, you'll find that many businesses that cater to tourists will accept euros, though they'll likely give you change in CHF. See p. 172 for information on money and costs.

Customs

Members of the European Union (E.U.) share many guidelines for arrivals. **Non-E.U. nationals aged 17 and over** can bring in 4 liters of wine and 16 liters of beer plus either 1 liter of alcohol more than 22% ("spirits") or 2 liters of "fortified" wine at less than 22%. Visitors may also bring in other goods, including perfume, gifts, and souvenirs, totaling 430€ in value. (Customs officials tend to be lenient about these general merchandise regulations, realizing the limits are unrealistically low.) Tobacco regulations vary by country, although an import limit of 200 cigarettes and 50 cigars is typical. For **arrivals from within the E.U.,** there are no limits as long as goods are for your own personal use, or are gifts. You can find details on Customs and excise rules for anyone entering the E.U. at **www.ec.europa. eu/taxation_ customs/common/ travellers**.

For specifics on what you can take home and the corresponding fees, U.S. citizens should download the free pamphlet *Know Before You Go* at **www.cbp.gov**. Alternatively, contact the **U.S. Customs & Border Protection (CBP),** 1300 Pennsylvania Ave. N.W., Washington, D.C. 20229 (© **877/CBP-5511**), and request the pamphlet. For a clear summary of their own rules, Canadians should consult the booklet *I Declare*, issued by the **Canada Border Services Agency** (www.cbsa-asfc. gc.ca; ℂ **800/461-9999** in Canada, or 204/983-3500). Australians need to read *Guide for Travellers: Know Before You Go*. For more information, call the **Australian Customs Service** at ℂ **1300/363-263,** or check **www.customs.gov. au/individuals**. For New Zealanders, most questions are answered under "Coming into NZ" at **www.customs. govt.nz**. For more information, contact the **New Zealand Customs Service** (ℂ **0800/428-786,** or 09/927-8036).

Doctors & Dentists Should you become seriously ill, lists of local doctors, dentists,

and hospitals can be found in telephone directories or by contacting your consulate, who have lists of English-speaking practitioners. Ask your hotel reception to help, or, in a real medical emergency, dial ℂ **144.**

Electricity Switzerland uses the 220-volt system (two round prongs). Always bring suitable transformers and/or adapters, such as world multiplugs—if you plug some American appliances directly into an electrical outlet without a transformer, for example, you'll destroy your appliance and possibly start a fire. Portable electronic devices such as iPods and mobile phones, however, recharge without problems via USB or using a multiplug. Many long-distance

European trains have plugs, for the charging of laptops and mobile phones.

Embassies & Consulates If your passport is stolen or lost, or if you are robbed, arrested, or become seriously ill while on vacation, your embassy or nearest consulate should be your first point of contact. While an embassy won't replace lost items (other than passports or national identity cards), bail you out of jail, or pay your plane fare home, it can refer you to English-speaking attorneys, doctors, or others who can assist in a crisis.

Australia: Chemins des Fins 2, Geneva; www.geneva. mission.gov.au; ℂ **22/799-9100.**

Canada: 5, avenue de l'Ariana, Geneva; www.switzerland.

gc.ca; ✆ **22/ 919-9200.**

New Zealand: Grand Saconnex, Geneva; E-mail: mission.nz@bluewin. ch; ✆ **22/929-0350.**

United Kingdom: Thunstrasse 50, Berne; www.gov.uk/ government/world/ switzerland; ✆ **031/ 359-7700.**

United States: 7 rue François-Versonnex, Geneva; www.bern.us embassy.gov; ✆ **22/840-5160.**

For questions about American citizens who are arrested abroad, including ways of getting money to them, telephone the **Citizens Emergency Center** of the Office of Special Consular Services in Washington, D.C. (✆ **202/ 647-5225**).

Emergencies
Dial ✆ **117** for police; ✆ **144** for an ambulance; and

✆ **118** to report a fire.

Internet & Wi-Fi
Wi-Fi is available at all but the most bare-bones of hotels (and usually at those, too). It's usually free, though oddly, some of the more expensive hotels charge needless daily fees for Wi-Fi. You'll find free or fee-based Wi-Fi hotspots in most cities' down-town areas, as well as at airports and train stations. If you're not connecting with your own laptop, tablet, or smartphone and need to find a local internet cafe, start by checking **www. cybercafes.com**. Although such places have suffered due to the spread of smartphones and free Wi-Fi (see below), they do tend to be prevalent close to popular tourist spots, especially ones

frequented by backpackers.

To locate free Wi-Fi hotspots, it's try using the hotspot locator at **www. hotspot-locations. com**. It's worth asking the local tourist office, too. They will likely be able to point you toward local providers where you can surf for free, or for the price of a cup of coffee at most. Many **long-distance trains,** especially on high-speed net-works, have onboard Wi-Fi.

Medical Requirements
Unless you're arriving from an area known to be suffering from an epi-demic (particularly cholera or yellow fever), inoculations or vaccinations are not required for entry into Europe.

Mobile Phones
The three letters that define much of the world's wireless

capabilities are **GSM** (Global System for Mobiles), a satellite network that makes for easy cross-border mobile phone use throughout most of the planet, including all of Europe. Check with your home-based provider to see what it will cost you to use your phone and access data from overseas; many companies will let you purchase an **international calling/data plan** for 1 month (or longer, depending on your length of stay), then cancel it when you return home.

Another alternative if you own an unlocked GSM phone: buy a contract-free **SIM-only tariff** when you arrive. The SIM card will cost very little, but you will need to load it up with credit to make calls. A few familiar names (Vodafone,

T-Mobile, and Orange among them) have local network operators in a number of European countries; some operators appear in just one. Tariffs change constantly in response to the market and by country. There are phone and SIM card retailers on practically every high-street in every country, and pretty much whichever operator you go with, you will make substantial savings over roaming with your home SIM.

There are other options if you're visiting from overseas but don't own an unlocked GSM phone. For a short visit, **renting** a phone may be a good idea, and we suggest renting the handset before you leave home. North Americans can rent from **InTouch USA** (www.intouchusa.us; ☎ **800/872-7626** or

703/222-7161) or **iRoam** (www.iroam. com; ☎ **888/454-7626**). However, handset prices have fallen to a level where you can often buy a basic local **pay-as-you-go (PAYG) phone** for less than 1 week's handset rental. Prices at many European cellphone retailers start from under US$50 for a cheap model, and you can often find an entry level Android smartphone for around US$100. Buy one, use it while you're here, and recycle it on the way home. Unfortunately, per-minute charges for international calls to your home country can be high, so if you plan to do a lot of calling home, use a VoIP service such as **Skype** (www.skype. com) in conjunction with a Web connection. See "Internet & Wi-Fi," above.

Money & Costs

Frommer's lists exact prices in the local currency. Exchange rates can fluctuate wildly in the space of just a few weeks, so before departing consult a currency exchange website such as **www. xe.com** to check up-to-the-minute rates.

When it comes to obtaining foreign currency, please, **skip the currency exchange kiosks** in airports, train stations, and elsewhere. They give the poorest rates and charge exorbitant fees. Instead, order a small amount of foreign currency from your bank before leaving home, and then figure on using your debit card for the duration of your trip. ATMs will give you a favorable rate, and you can withdraw however much cash you need for a day or so, as opposed to

carrying around wads of money.

ATMs are everywhere in Switzerland—depending on the country, you'll find them at banks, city squares, some fuel stations, highway rest stops, supermarkets, post offices, or all of the above. The **Cirrus** (www.mastercard. com) and **PLUS** (www.visa.com) networks span the globe; look at the back of your bank card to see which network you're on, and then check online for ATM locations at your destination if you want to be ultra-organized. Be sure you know your personal identification number (PIN) and daily withdrawal limit before you depart. Confirm with your bank that your PIN will work in Europe, and be sure to let them know the dates and destinations to which you're traveling—

you don't want to find your card frozen while you're abroad! Credit cards are accepted just about everywhere, exept street markets, small independent retailers, street-food vendors, and occasional small or family-owned businesses. However, North American visitors should note that American Express is accepted far less widely than at home, and Diners Club Card only at the very highest of highflying establishments. To be sure of your credit line, bring a Visa or MasterCard as well.

Most retailers ask for your 4-digit PIN to be entered into a keypad near the cash register. In restaurants, a server might bring a handheld device to your table to authorize payment. If you're visiting from a country where Chip and PIN is less prevalent (such as the U.S.), it's possible that some retailers will be reluctant to accept your swipe cards. Be prepared to argue your case: Swipe cards are still valid, and the same machines that read the smartcard chips can also read your magnetic strip. However, do carry some cash with you too, just in case.

Passports & Visas To travel throughout Switzerland, all U.S. and British citizens, Canadians, Australians, and New Zealanders must have a passport valid through their length of stay. No visa is required. The immigration officer may also want to see proof of your intention to return to your point of origin (usually a round-trip ticket) and of visible means of support while you're in Europe. If you're planning to fly from the United States or Canada to Europe and then on to a country that requires a visa (India, for example), you should secure that visa before you depart.

Pharmacies

Swiss pharmacies dispense over-the-counter and prescription medicines. They are easily identifiable by the sign of a green cross on a white background. Regular hours are Monday to Saturday, from around 9am to 6pm. Major cities have at least one 24-hour pharmacy open. In Zurich, there's one near the lake at Bellevue (✆ **044/266 62 22;** in Geneva, call ✆ **144** to ask which pharmacy is on duty out of hours.

Post Offices

Switzerland's postal service (Swiss Post; www.post.ch; ✆ **0848-88 88 88**) is fast and reliable. Stamps can be purchased at post offices and some newspaper kiosks. Post office opening times are typically Monday to Friday 8:30am to 6:30pm, Saturday 8:30 to 11am, but main post offices (in Zurich at Europaallee 11, and I Geneva at Cornavin station, rue des Gares 16) are open longer hours.

Taxes All European countries charge a **value-added tax (VAT)** of between 8% and 25% on goods and services, with most hovering on the high side of 20%. Unlike a U.S. sales tax, it is already included in any store price you see quoted.

Citizens of non-E.U. countries can, as they leave the country, get back most of the tax on purchases (not services) if they spend above a designated amount (usually around $250) in a single store. Regulations vary from country to country, so inquire at the tourist office when you arrive to find out the procedure; ask what percentage of the tax is refunded, and whether the refund is given to you at the airport or mailed to you later. Look for a **tax free shopping for tourists** sign posted in participating stores. Always ask the storekeeper for the necessary forms, and keep the purchases in their original packages if you want them to be valid for a VAT refund. Save your receipts and VAT forms from each E.U. country to process all of them at your final exit point from the E.U. (allow an extra 30 min. or so at an airport to process forms).

To avoid VAT refund hassles, when leaving an E.U. country for the last leg of your trip, take your goods, receipts, and passport to have the form stamped by Customs. Then take all your documentation to the VAT Refund counter you'll find at hundreds of airports and border crossings. Your money is refunded on the spot. For more information, contact **Global Blue** (www. global-blue.com).

Time Switzerland observes CET (Central European Time), and is 6 hours ahead of New York. For instance, when it's noon in New York, it's 6pm in Lucerne or Geneva. European countries all observe daylight saving time, but the time change doesn't usually occur on the same day as in

North America or the Southern Hemisphere countries. There's plenty of extra guidance at **www.timeanddate. com**.

Tipping The cultural ins-and-outs of tipping vary widely across Europe. And indeed, the whole concept of tipping isn't without controversy: Some Europeans, for example, resent a "tipping culture being imported" from North America and elsewhere—the practice, where it exists, is nowhere near as ingrained as it is in the U.S. There are, however, a few instances when a tip is appreciated, no matter where you are. In grand hotels, tip **bellhops** around 1€ per bag and tip the **chamber staff,** too, if you like—though it's not expected in most establishments. In family-run hotels, it's not always considered polite to leave anything at all. Tip the **doorman** or **concierge** of a grand hotel only if he or she has provided you with some specific service (for example, obtaining difficult-to-get theater tickets). If you come across **valet-parking,** tip the attendant 1€ when your car arrives.

In restaurants, tip **service staff** 10% of the check if you feel the service has warranted it, though again this is by no means standard practice among locals "in Switzerland. Be sure to check if a **service charge** has already been applied; if it has, there's no need to leave more. **Bar staff** expect nothing, unless you're in a very high-toned nightspot, when you should round up and add a euro or two. **Cab drivers** may expect a euro or two on top of the fare, especially if they have helped with your luggage—though luggage fees often apply anyway, so don't feel obliged. **Hairdressers** and **barbers** also appreciate an extra euro or so for a job well done.

Index

ACCOMMODATIONS

RESTAURANTS

PHOTO CREDITS

p. iii: Oscity / Shutterstock.com; p. 1: Alessandro Colle; p. 4-5: © Michael Portmann; p. 8: © Zürich Tourism / Martin Rütschi; p. 10: S.Borisov; p. 14: eGuide Travel; p. 15: Andreas Zerndl / Shutterstock.com; p. 18: Rudy Balasko; p. 19: Ethan Prater; p. 22: Courtesy of Landesmuseum Zürich; p. 24: TTstudio; p. 27: Matyas Rehak; p. 28: photogearch / Shutterstock.com; p. 30: Alexander Chaikin; p. 33: Courtesy of Widder Hotel; p. 35: Courtesy of The Hotel Bar Au Lac; p. 38: Allie_Caulfield; p. 42: Courtesy of Confiserie Sprunglei/ Karin Lurz; p. 44: Yusuke Kawasaki; p. 48-49: Oscity / Shutterstock.com; p. 50: kuhnmi; p. 53: Leonid Andronov; p. 54: Boris-B / Shutterstock.com; p. 63: Philip Pilosian / Shutterstock.com; p. 67: Martin Good / Shutterstock.com; p. 68: In Green / Shutterstock.com; p. 71: b-hide the scene; p. 72: Boris-B; p. 73: Jack at Wikipedia; p. 74: ©RicardoDeLaRiva/ Geneva Tourism & Convention Foundation; p. 78: Courtesy of Hotel Beau Rivage; p. 95: © Arnaud-Derib/ FONDATION DU FESTIVAL DE JAZZ DE MONTREUX; p. 96: Fedor Selivanov; p. 97: Bertl123; p. 100: Elge Kenneweg/ AURA/ Luzern Tourismus; p. 101: Boris Stroujko; p. 103: Simon; p. 107: Olgysha; p. 111: Marcin Wichary; p. 114: Courtesy of Hotel Schweizerhof Luzern; p. 116: jay8085; p. 119: Courtesy of Old Swiss House; p. 122: Courtesy of Kultur und Kongress Zentrum Lucerne; p. 124: © www.iglu-dorf. com; p. 126: anshar; p. 129: pinggr; p. 137: Courtesy of Unique Hotel Post; p. 141: Zermatt Tourismus/ © Iglu Dorf; p. 146-147: Nelson Minar; p. 150: © Michael Portmann.

ommer's
lt

FROMMER'S.COM

FROMMERS.COM IS KEPT UP-TO-DATE, WITH:

NEWS
The latest events (and deals) to affect your next vacation.

BLOGS
Opinionated comments by our outspoken staff

FORUMS
Post your travel questions, get answers from other readers

SLIDESHOWS
On weekly-changing, practical but inspiring topics of travel

CONTESTS
Enabling you to win free trips

PODCASTS
Of our weekly, nationwide radio show

DESTINATIONS
Hundreds of cities, their hotels, restaurants and sights

TRIP IDEAS
Valuable, offbeat suggestions for your next vacation

*AND MUCH MORE!

Smart travelers consult Frommers.com